Best Behavior

Building Positive Behavior Support in Schools

Jeffrey Sprague
Annemieke Golly

SOPRIS WEST Educational Services
A Cambium Learning Company

BOSTON, MA • NEW YORK, NY • LONGMONT, CO

ISBN 1-59318-071-3

The authors wish to extend their appreciation to Stephen Smith of the University of Oregon IVDB for his extensive contributions to Chapter 8.

09 08 07 06 05   6 5 4 3 2

Printed in the United States of America
Published and Distributed by

SOPRIS
WEST
EDUCATIONAL SERVICES

4093 Specialty Place • Longmont, Colorado 80504
(303) 651-2829 • www.sopriswest.com

230BEST/5-05/BAN

Acknowledgments

The research, techniques, and ideas in this guide represent many years of hard work in schools for us, first as classroom teachers, and later as consultants, trainers, and researchers. We are gratefully indebted to many of our mentors, colleagues, and friends for their support and innovative ideas, and their enthusiasm for helping school personnel, families, and students lead happier and more successful lives during their school years and beyond.

We have had many mentors at the University of Oregon. We thank Hill Walker for his superb expertise as a researcher and mentor of so many leaders in our field, and for being an excellent friend and colleague. His mentorship, quiet guidance, and passion for improving the lives of children is a beacon for all of us.

We also thank Rob Horner and George Sugai for their amazing leadership and insight regarding methods and systems for implementing schoolwide behavioral support and functional behavioral assessment. The opportunity to collaborate with them to develop and refine many of the methods in this guide has been an honor and a pleasure, and we look forward to many more years of collaboration and shared learning.

One of the markers of the outstanding research success at the University of Oregon is our superb colleague group. We work with several amazing colleagues who through their work give us new ideas and shape our thinking and practice daily.

We give a special thanks to our colleague Geoff Colvin for his superb work on defusing behavioral escalation and his ability to help us all interpret and solve complex teacher–student interactions in ways that make them seem simple.

Sincere thanks also to our colleague Stephen Smith of the University of Oregon IVDB, who is the lead author on Chapter 8 (Active Supervision of Common Areas). His excellent work in helping educators more effectively supervise students provides an essential component to positive behavior supports in schools.

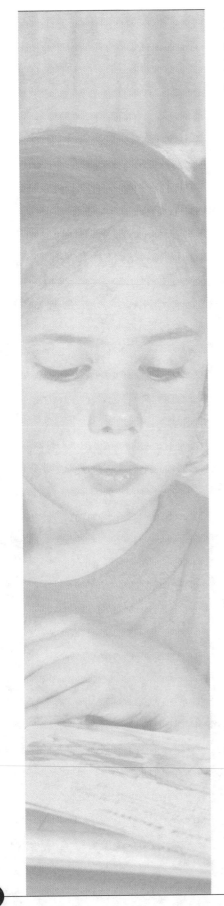

Finally, we wish to thank our colleagues in the schools for their commitment to improving school discipline systems and the lives of students. They also guide our work and help us make it as good as it can be!

About the Authors

Jeffrey Sprague, Ph.D., is an associate professor of special education and codirector of the University of Oregon Institute on Violence and Destructive Behavior. In 2001, Dr. Sprague worked with the Oregon legislature to establish the Oregon Center for School Safety. He was a classroom teacher for seven years and a school behavioral consultant for two years. He directs federal, state, and local research and demonstration projects related to schoolwide discipline, youth violence prevention, alternative education services, juvenile delinquency prevention, and school systems change. His research activities encompass applied behavior analysis, positive behavior supports, functional behavioral assessment, school safety and violence prevention, and juvenile delinquency. Jeff is a contributor to "Early Warning, Timely Response" and the 1998, 1999, and 2000 *Annual Reports on School Safety*. Most recently, he has written a book on crime prevention through environmental design for school administrators. Jeff is co-author with Hill Walker on a book about school safety to be published by Guilford Publications (in press).

Annemieke Golly, Ph.D., is a certified special education teacher who has taught children with behavior and conduct disorders for the past 20 years. Dr. Golly received her Ph.D. in special education at the University of Oregon. Her areas of expertise are preventive interventions, behavior management, and classroom and schoolwide management. She is currently working at the Institute on Violence and Destructive Behavior at the University of Oregon as a teacher/trainer as well as program director and coordinator for First Step to Success, an early intervention program to divert children from a path of antisocial behavior.

She has been a coordinator for designing and implementing schoolwide violence prevention programs, and has worked as a consultant/trainer to implement behavior management strategies in the United States, Canada, the Virgin Islands, the Netherlands, Germany, and South Africa. She has taught numerous university courses and school district, teacher, and parent training courses. She is co-author of the book *Why Johnny Doesn't Behave: 20 Tips for Measurable BIPs*.

Contents

List of Reproducibles

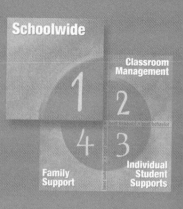

Schoolwide

Classroom Management

1 2
4 3

Family Support

Individual Student Supports

Schoolwide Positive Behavior Supports

chapter 1

Welcome to *Best Behavior*

Chapter Objectives:

○ Describe what *Best Behavior* provides

○ Describe why *Best Behavior* is needed to improve discipline in schools

○ Discuss how to use this guide

This integrated system of schoolwide, classroom management, and individual student supports is designed to give you simple but effective tactics and strategies to improve behavioral outcomes for the students you serve and their families. With this guide, you will gain a variety of new skills and knowledge that are based on the best research available.

Two issues are constant challenges to effective education: academic achievement and discipline. Students who are not safe, respectful, and responsible in schools impede the learning process for others. School personnel who do not work together and focus on outcomes will be frustrated, inconsistent, and ineffective. Parents who are not supported and encouraged to collaborate will feel left out and their children will not do as well in school. We will spend time together learning the most recent research-validated and evidence-based techniques for establishing a positive school climate where no child is left behind and no teacher is left unsupported.

What *Best Behavior* Provides

Best Behavior provides proven, effective management methods for students in school common areas (*all* students in the school), for those at risk of behavior problems (*some* students), and for the (*few*) students in your school who are already disruptive and undisciplined. This integrated approach has been shown to be effective in research (Walker et al., 1996) but has only recently been broadly adopted by schools and school systems. Without an integrated approach to melding school, classroom, and individual student supports, schools often use effective strategies in a piecemeal and inconsistent fashion.

Best Behavior provides a standardized staff development program aimed at improving school and classroom discipline and reducing associated outcomes such as school violence and alcohol, tobacco, and other drug use. It is based on the Positive Behavioral Support (PBS) approach (Sprague, Sugai, & Walker, 1998; Sprague et al., 2001; Sugai & Horner, 1994) developed at the University of Oregon and the National Center on Positive Behavioral Interventions and Supports (www.pbis.org), an Office of Special Education Programs–funded research center. The goal of *Best Behavior* is to facilitate the academic achievement and healthy social development of children and youth in a safe environment that is conducive to learning.

> *Best Behavior* addresses schoolwide, classroom, and individual student interventions, as well as family collaboration, and it is one of the few programs that offers supports for *all* students in the school, *some* students with additional needs, and the *few* students who need the most intensive supports (as outlined in Chapter 3).

Evidence Based

Best Behavior includes intervention techniques based on over 30 years of rigorous research in school discipline from the education, public health, psychology, and criminology fields (Greenberg, Domitrovich, & Bumbarger, 1999; Walker et al., 1996). Program components address schoolwide, common area, classroom, and individual student interventions and are intended to be used in combination with other evidence-based prevention programs, such as the Second Step violence prevention curriculum (Committee for Children, 1997) or Life Skills Training (Botvan, 1979).

Effective

Best Behavior and similar approaches (see Mayer & Sulzer-Azaroff, 1990 or Sprick, Sprick, & Garrison, 1992a, 1992b) have been tested and applied by other researchers and practitioners using the same and similar techniques. The effects of the program are documented in a series of studies conducted by researchers at the University of Oregon and elsewhere (Metzler, Biglan, Rusby, & Sprague, 2001; Sprague et al., 2001; Taylor-Greene et al., 1997; see also www.pbis.org for the latest research studies and reports on positive behavior supports). Studies using *Best Behavior* have shown reductions in office discipline referrals of up to 50 percent, with continued improvement over a three-year period in schools that sustain the intervention (Irvin, Tobin, Sprague, & Vincent, in press). In addition, school staff report greater satisfaction with their work compared to schools that did not implement *Best Behavior*. Comparison schools show increases or no change in office referrals, along with general frustration with the school discipline program (Sprague et al.).

In studies employing some or all of the components included in *Best Behavior*, reductions have been documented in antisocial behavior (Sprague et al., 2001), vandalism (Mayer, 1995), aggression (Grossman et al. 1997; Lewis, Sugai, & Colvin, 1998), later delinquency (Kellam, Mayer, Rebok, & Hawkins, 1998; O'Donnell, Hawkins, Catalano, & Abbott, 1995), and alcohol, tobacco, and other drug use (Metzler et al., 2001; O'Donnell et al.). Positive changes in protective factors such as academic achievement (Kellam et al.; O'Donnell et al.) and school engagement (O'Donnell et al.) have been documented using a positive school discipline program as set out in this book and in concert with other prevention interventions.

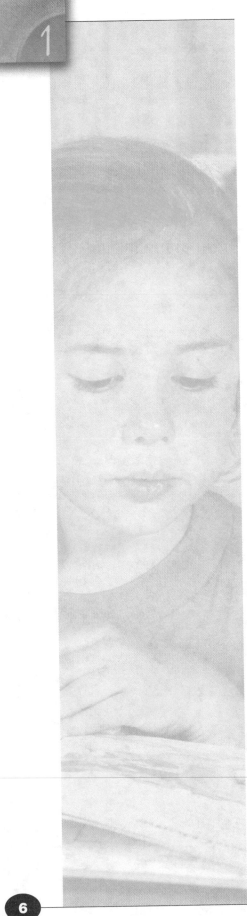

How *Best Behavior* Will Help You

The following points outline the key methods you can expect to learn from *Best Behavior*.

Improve Schoolwide Practices

You will learn to:

- Carry out strategies for improving the consistency and effectiveness of school discipline systems. We recommend that every school employ a representative team to implement each strategy in this guide.

- Assess the current status and needs of your school regarding discipline and safety and use that assessment to set goals. Interventions are more effective if they are based on a comprehensive and representative needs assessment.

- Develop a plan for choosing and teaching school rules and behavior expectations. Schools should use a small number of clear, positively stated rules to guide students and teachers alike.

- Develop a plan to directly teach expected behavior in your school. Students must be regularly taught expected behavior to assure maintenance.

- Develop a plan to actively supervise all students in common areas such as hallways, cafeterias, and playgrounds. Much problem behavior occurs in common areas of the school. *Best Behavior* outlines a simple but powerful strategy for improving common-area supervision.

- Use office discipline referral patterns and other data to continuously improve and share success with all adults in the school. School personnel perform better and "buy in" to program improvement if they get regular feedback on discipline patterns in the school.

- Work to build and sustain effective management practices in your school. Improving school discipline is an ongoing process.

- Achieve consistency between classroom and schoolwide discipline procedures. As schoolwide procedures are established, you link them to your classroom management routines and practices.

Improve Classroom Management Effectiveness

You will learn to:

- Decrease student misbehavior in the classroom. Prevent problems before they start by using your own behavior strategically.

- Effectively and consistently gain student attention. Using clear signals in the classroom minimizes disruption.

- Use effective systems to reward and maintain expected behavior. Students need clear, consistent encouragement.

- Foster cooperative, respectful, and responsible behavior between students by directly teaching and providing positive and corrective feedback. Predictable problems in classrooms can be solved by preventive teaching.

- Directly teach and support positive student social skills in the classroom. Expected behaviors need to be taught and reviewed.

Improve Support Systems for Individual Students

You will learn to:

- Objectively assess the reasons for student misbehavior and develop positive support plans for individual students. Thinking functionally about behavior will increase your effectiveness.

- Respond effectively to harassment, noncompliance, and escalating behavior. Use your behavior to defuse these challenges.

- Teach students to self-manage their behavior and learning. Self-control and intrinsic motivation are taught using simple procedures.

Collaborate Effectively With All Parents in the School

You will learn to:

- Develop strategies for positive communication with families. It is critical to inform families of your school-wide and classroom procedures.

- Collaborate with parents to support healthy and safe behavior at home and school. Parents are valuable partners in promoting student success.

Why Do Schools Need *Best Behavior*?

Many school practices contribute to the development of antisocial behavior and the potential for violence in schools. Because it has been common to place responsibility for behavior change on individual students or their families, such school practices are often overlooked as factors in a behavior problem. They include:

- Ineffective instruction that results in academic failure.

- Failure to individualize instruction to adapt to individual differences.

- Inconsistent and punitive schoolwide, classroom, and individual behavior management practices.

- Lack of opportunity to learn and practice prosocial interpersonal and self-management skills.

- Unclear rules and expectations regarding expected behavior in all school settings.

- Failure to correct rule violations in a firm but fair manner that emphasizes teaching rather than retribution.

- Failure to help students from at-risk backgrounds adjust to the schooling process.

- Failure to encourage active collaboration and cooperation with parents and families.

- Failure to sustain and consistently implement positive behavior support practices.

These factors are *all* amenable to change with a broad-based preventive approach (Mayer, 1995; Sprague et al., 2001; Sugai & Horner, 1994; Walker et al., 1996). Unfortunately, school personnel have a long history of applying simple and unproven solutions (e.g., office discipline referrals, suspensions) to complex behavior problems. They express understandable disappointment when these attempts do not work as expected (Walker et al., 1996). This practice is sustained by a tendency to try to remove the problem student via office referrals, suspension, or expulsion, rather than finding a way to reduce the administrative, teaching, and management practices that have contributed to the problem (Tobin, Sugai, & Martin, 2000).

How Do We Solve This Problem?

Educators in today's schools and classrooms must be supported to adopt and sustain effective, cost-efficient practices (Sugai & Horner, 1994; Walker et al., 1996). This approach, referred to as Positive Behavior Supports, includes (1) systematic social skills instruction; (2) academic and curricular restructuring; (3) positive, behaviorally based interventions; (4) early screening and identification for antisocial behavior patterns; and (5) preventive schoolwide discipline (Sprague, Sugai, & Walker, 1998; Sugai & Horner; Walker et al.).

Using This Guide

The materials included in this guide are designed to be used for both your own practice and to support team-based training. The best results are obtained when all adults in the school use the practices, all students are affected, and data are used continually to improve and sustain each school system (e.g., schoolwide, classroom, individual student) and intervention method (e.g., school rule teaching, self-management). Chapter 2 will outline our approach to providing team-based staff development.

Best Behavior is organized into four sections: (1) Schoolwide Positive Behavior Supports, (2) Classroom Management, (3) Individual Student Supports, and (4) Family Support. Each chapter is designed to be used to support team-based staff development at the building or school district level.

Chapter 2: **Best Behavior** ***Staff Development: What It Looks Like***. This chapter describes the logistics of the staff development and technical assistance program. We outline recommended start-up procedures and tasks and provide sample training agendas to illustrate the approach.

Chapter 3: Introduction to the Challenge of Antisocial Behavior. We begin this chapter by outlining the challenge of school violence and discipline problems. It is of critical importance for educators to understand the prevalence of destructive life outcomes for children who are antisocial if they are not given positive behavior supports. We close by providing a review of evidence-based effective practices. Knowledge of what works and what doesn't can guide you and your school team as you build and implement your interventions.

Chapter 4: School Organization: Getting Started With **Best Behavior**. In this chapter we describe the components of a schoolwide positive behavior support system. Conducting a needs assessment is the first step in program development recommended by No Child Left Behind, and we present a self-assessment of the essential practices in your school and ask you to identify priorities for intervention. You will also develop three to four annual goals into an action plan.

Chapter 5: Defining Schoolwide Behavior Expectations. In this chapter you will learn how to define the behavior expectations (i.e., compliance to adult requests, positive peer-to-peer interactions, academic effort, and school safety) for your school and communicate them to all adults and students.

Chapter 6: Teaching Schoolwide Behavior Expectations. In this chapter you will learn the basics of teaching and communicating behavioral expectations and develop a sample lesson plan for teaching them. We present practical methods for increasing consistency of rule teaching and making it fun for both adults and students. As you consider adoption of research-validated social skills curricula such as the Second Step violence prevention curriculum (Committee for Children, 1997) or Life

Skills Training (Botvan, 1979), you will find that the recommendations in this chapter provide an excellent foundation for maximizing their effectiveness.

Chapter 7: Schoolwide Recognition and Reward Systems: Creating a Positive School Culture. In this chapter we list the components of effective reward systems, discuss facts and fiction about positive reinforcement, and present ideas for increasing consistency among the adults in the school. You also have the opportunity to build a schoolwide recognition and reward system.

Chapter 8: Active Supervision of Common Areas. Common areas such as cafeterias, playgrounds, or hallways are often overlooked as the source of many behavioral problems in schools. In this chapter we present four essential techniques of active supervision, including: (1) positive contacts with students, (2) positive reinforcement, (3) scanning and movement, and (4) correcting behavioral errors. We present a method for planning a strategy to make your common areas safer and more positive.

Chapter 9: Using Discipline Referrals to Diagnose Schoolwide and Individual Student Needs. Sprague, Sugai, Horner, and Walker (1999) suggest that analyzing office discipline referral patterns in schools provides a simple but useful source of data to make decisions about the effectiveness of schoolwide, classroom, common area, and individual student interventions. In this chapter we describe features of a good discipline referral system, provide model discipline referral forms, and offer a set of decision rules to detect school program improvement needs.

Chapter 10: Classroom Organization: The Foundation of Classroom Management. Chapter 10 is the beginning of a comprehensive approach to improving classroom management effectiveness. The techniques are simple and powerful when implemented consistently across classrooms in your school. We describe the organization of an effective classroom and provide a checklist to evaluate your classroom environment. You will be asked to set goals for improving your classroom environment.

Chapter 11: Designing and Teaching Classroom Behavioral Expectations. We recommend linking schoolwide behavior expectations and routines to those used in your classroom. As teachers, you have unique routines and expectations that fit your classroom and teaching practices. In this chapter we will

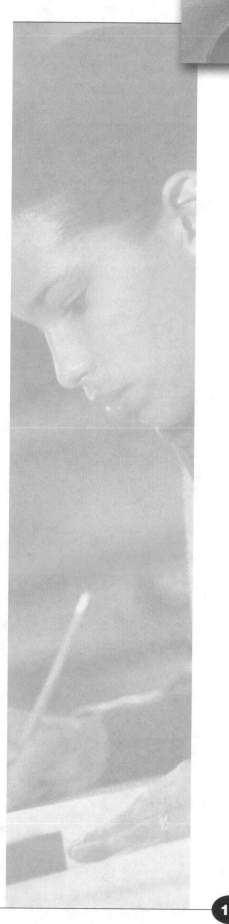

guide you to develop a few, positive classroom rules that are linked to the schoolwide system. We also describe how teaching and encouraging compliance to classroom rules contribute to effective classroom management.

Chapter 12: Preventive Interactions. If we want to change a student's behavior, we must change our own behavior. This chapter presents some very useful preventive interactions that can minimize problem behavior in your classroom. You will learn to use a consistent attention signal for the whole class and to use direct speech when giving instructions to students. We will teach you to present a specific predictable request sequence to noncompliant students and show you how to teach an on-task routine called the Concentration/Focus Power Game to use during disruptions.

Chapter 13: Using Consequences to Change Group and Individual Behavior. Effective teachers use a combination of positive reinforcement for expected behavior and firm but fair corrections for behavioral errors. In this chapter you will identify positive consequences to use in your classroom as well as effective corrective consequences. You will also design integrated motivational systems to teach and reinforce positive behavior change.

Chapter 14: Responding to Escalating Behavior and Verbal Harassment. Escalating behavior and verbal harassment exhibited by students seriously impact proper functioning of a school and classroom. Behaviors such as aggression, severe disruption, and acting-out can cause major problems for adults and students in terms of personal safety and stress, and significantly disrupt the teaching and learning processes in school. In this chapter we identify common assumptions that get teachers into power struggles and suggest procedures to de-escalate behaviors.

Chapter 15: Thinking Functionally About Behavior. Behavioral approaches to school and classroom management provide some of the most effective solutions to reducing problem behavior. Functional Behavioral Assessment (FBA) methods (O'Neill et al., 1997) provide an easy way to assess the motivation behind problem behavior and link our response logically to that motivation. In this chapter you will learn to define functional behavioral assessment, list the outcomes of a complete functional behavioral assessment, describe information needed for a functional behavioral assessment, and discuss the logical link between functional behavioral assessment outcomes and positive support plan procedures. Thinking functionally works for special education students as well as typical students.

Chapter 16: Building Positive Behavior Support Plans for Challenging Students. We need to develop positive support plans that fit our skills, values, and resources. In this chapter you will learn to describe the logical link from functional assessment results to positive supports and discuss what changes adults can make to bring about change in student behavior. Positive behavior support plans help us make problem behaviors irrelevant, ineffective, and inefficient by teaching and encouraging replacement behaviors.

Chapter 17: Adapting Curricula to Prevent Problem Behavior. One of the principal reasons that students misbehave in school is instruction that is too difficult or poorly adapted. In this chapter you will learn to use instructional and curriculum adaptation to help students become more successful and behave better. You will learn to describe classes of adaptation that can prevent problem behavior, outline a process for adapting curricula and instruction, and develop and adapt a classroom lesson to prevent problem behavior.

Chapter 18: Teaching Students Who Are At Risk to Self-Manage Their Behavior. Many of us hope that our students will become self-directed, intrinsically motivated learners. Walker (1995) indicates that teachers value compliance to reasonable requests and students who are prepared for class and do their best to complete assigned work. Safe, respectful, and responsible students learn to self-manage their behavior. In this chapter we describe the purposes and benefits of teaching self-management, describe the core features of self-management programs, and illustrate how to design and teach a self-management program.

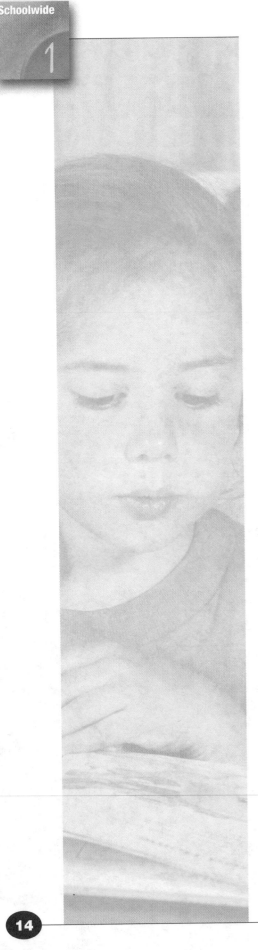

Chapter 19: School/Home Collaboration. Parents are key partners in supporting school success and encouraging expected behaviors from their children. This chapter provides you with ideas and resources to communicate and work cooperatively with parents and/or caregivers. The first part of the chapter provides tips and effective strategies for teachers. The second part outlines effective parenting practices and includes reproducible sheets for parents to use.

Conclusion: Planning to Sustain and Improve Your Success. In the conclusion we ask you to reflect on your learning and set goals for continued improvement of practices in your school.

Personalizing Your Learning
From *Best Behavior*

Please take a few minutes to write down your thoughts before you begin *Best Behavior*.

1. Things I would like to learn about effective positive behavior support practices are . . .

_____

_____

_____

2. The most frustrating behavior I encounter is . . .

_____

_____

_____

3. If I could have any resources for supporting a student, they would be . . .

_____

_____

_____

4. Things that work when dealing with problem behavior are . . .

_____

_____

_____

5. Things that don't work when dealing with problem behavior are . . .

_____

_____

_____

6. Some ways to improve discipline consistency in my school are . . .

_____

_____

_____

7. Some roadblocks to gaining discipline consistency in my school are . . .

_____

_____

_____

chapter 2

Best Behavior Staff Development: What It Looks Like

Chapter Objectives:

❍ Describe the format and logistics of *Best Behavior* staff development

❍ Outline time requirements for successful implementation

❍ Illustrate a sample training schedule

To install and maintain each of the *Best Behavior* components, representative teams of teachers are trained and supported over a two- to three-year period. These school teams work to complete initial and ongoing needs assessments, choose interventions (e.g., school rules, social skills curricula), and use student- and staff-level data to refine and evaluate their efforts. All of the materials needed for implementation are contained in this guide; additional consumable forms and evaluation materials are provided at the training events.

Representative school team members are trained to develop and implement positive school rules, rule teaching, positive reinforcement systems, data-based decision making at the school level,

effective classroom management methods, curriculum adaptation to prevent problem behavior, and functional behavioral assessment and positive behavioral supports. Teams are also coached to integrate *Best Behavior* with other prevention programs to maximize effectiveness.

How Does This Fit in the Big Picture of School Improvement?

We recommend that every school include improvement of discipline and safety as a top priority and that at least 85 percent of staff formally indicate commitment to the training and implementation process. Administrative leadership is emphasized throughout the process. The building administrator is required to be part of the school discipline team and to participate in all planning and staff development activities.

The school team should include a representative from each major stakeholder group (e.g., grade-level teachers, classified personnel, administration, and parents). Once implementation goals are set, all school stakeholders should receive training and information. Dates and format for schoolwide training need to be planned during normal staff release days, or funding needs to be provided to support these activities. We suggest that funding for staff release or stipends for participation be provided for building discipline team members.

How Do I Know If It Is Working?

Participating schools are asked to develop and present an annual plan with measurable goals and objectives. The goal-setting session is conducted early in the process (see Chapter 4) and is refined over the course of the training or during in-building meetings.

Student measures may include knowledge change on social skills teaching, discipline referral patterns, achievement test scores, attendance, etc. We also recommend using staff and student surveys to measure progress.

How Much Time Is Involved?

Training sessions are delivered sequentially, and each of the 20 segments is designed to last approximately one to one and a half hours, for a total training time of 18–25 hours. Each segment can be delivered alone, in four one-day sessions, or in 15–20 separate, distributed training sessions. Figure 1 provides a sample four-day training agenda. Our experience is that longer sessions (half day or full day) are most productive for school teams, and we recommend that the four days be separated from each other by at least one month. It is typical for us to work with school teams for two consecutive days, and then return one to three months later for the third and fourth day. This lets teams get the initial work going and allows time to try early strategies and return with "on the ground" questions.

While participating in training and after completion of the basic material, we recommend that school discipline teams meet approximately once per month to review training content as needed and to set up a regular process of reviewing and refining the school discipline plan (initial goals are developed during training) and other, school site-based activities. A format for these meetings is specified in training, and each meeting should last 20–60 minutes.

Figure 1

Sample *Best Behavior* Training Agenda

Day 1
**Schoolwide Positive
Behavior Supports**

1—Welcome to Best Behavior

2—Best Behavior Staff Development:
What It Looks Like

3—Introduction to the Challenge of
Antisocial Behavior

4—School Organization: Getting Started
with *Best Behavior*

5—Defining Schoolwide Behavior
Expectations

Day 2
**Schoolwide Positive Behavior
Supports and Classroom
Management**

6—Teaching Schoolwide Behavior
Expectations

7—Schoolwide Recognition and Reward
Systems: Creating a Positive School
Culture

8—Active Supervision of Common Areas

9—Using Discipline Referrals to
Diagnose Schoolwide and Individual
Student Needs

10—Classroom Organization: The
Foundation of Classroom Management

Day 3
**Classroom Management and
Individual Student Supports**

11—Designing and Teaching Classroom
Behavioral Expectations

12—Preventive Interactions

13—Using Consequences to Change
Group and Individual Behavior

14—Responding to Escalating Behavior
and Verbal Harassment

Day 4
**Individual Student Supports and
Family Support**

15—Thinking Functionally About
Behavior

16—Building Positive Behavior Support
Plans for Challenging Students

17—Adapting Curricula to Prevent
Problem Behavior

18—Teaching Students Who Are At Risk
to Self-Manage Their Behavior

19—School/Home Collaboration

Conclusion—Planning to Sustain and
Improve Your Success

chapter 3

Introduction to the Challenge of Antisocial Behavior

Chapter Objectives:

○ Outline the need for positive behavior supports in schools

○ Describe how challenging behavior develops through a student's life

○ Outline an integrated approach to addressing the problem of challenging behavior in schools

The purpose of this chapter is to describe a fully integrated, comprehensive approach to preventing problem and challenging behavior in schools—an approach that may have a better chance to work than other, more traditional approaches. Specifically, we outline a school-based approach to the prevention of challenging, aggressive behavior patterns that: (1) targets the entire school site as well as individual students for assessment and intervention, (2) matches the intensity and nature of interventions with the severity and intractability of students' adjustment problems, and (3) emphasizes the fostering of prosocial and safe learning environments for all students.

Antisocial Behavior in Schools

Schools often reflect societal trends in the rise of interpersonal violence and conflict. The following statistics and observations illustrate the declining quality of life in schools:

- Thousands of students bring weapons to school each day, and some are killed or wounded with these weapons each year.

- Large numbers of students fear victimization on the way to and from school.

- More than one in five students in our nation's schools are afraid to use school bathrooms because they are often sites for assaults and other forms of victimization.

- Thousands of teachers are threatened, assaulted, or injured in schools each year.

- Students are increasingly intimidated and threatened by mean-spirited teasing, bullying, and sexual harassment occurring at school.

- Schools are sites for recruitment and related activities by organized gangs.

    (Committee for Children, 1996; National School Safety Center, 1996; Office of Juvenile Justice and Delinquency Program [OJJDP], 1995; Walker, Colvin, & Ramsey, 1995)

While we may get the impression that schools and children are out of control, schools are in fact relatively safe places for children. The statistics in Figure 2 represent research-based estimates of the prevalence of violent and challenging behavior in schools. The evidence indicates that a small number of students are contributing to most serious problems in schools. While most students in schools will respond positively to well-organized classrooms, clear behavior expectations, and rich, positive reinforcement (Sprague et al., 2001), we also need to add specialized supports for those who do not improve with the schoolwide program alone.

Figure 2

How Prevalent Is the Problem?

- 8–12% of school-age children and youth have conduct problems (American Psychological Association, 1993).

- 12–22% of youth under 18 have adjustment problems that require mental health services (U.S. Department of Health and Human Services, 2001).

- 5% of Lane County, Oregon youth (ages 10–17) had a Youth Services referral in 2002—20% of offenders committed 87% of all new crime.

- 6–9% of children in schools account for more than 50% of discipline referrals (Sprague, Sugai, et al., 1999; Sugai et al., 2000).

Identify Students With Extra Support Needs Early

Students who display chronic challenging and violent behavior are on a "risk pathway" to short- and long-term negative outcomes. The root of these problems often originates in the family and community through chronic and long-term exposure to key risk factors—experiences that make negative outcomes more likely for a child. When children come to school, the development of challenging behavior is actually increased because children encounter additional structure, demands, and peer interactions.

We also have learned that children with the most serious problems do not "grow out of it." Instead, they tend to become challenging adults who continue to have adjustment problems. Figure 3 outlines a classic pattern of challenging behavioral development and illustrates the complexity of the pathway as conceptualized by Gerald Patterson and his associates (Loeber & Farrington, 1998; Patterson, Reid, & Dishion, 1992; Sprague & Walker, 2000).

The Risk Path to Antisocial Behavior

Exposure to Family, Neighborhood School, and Societal Risk Factors

poverty, abuse, and neglect; harsh and inconsistent parenting; drug and alcohol use by caregivers; emotional and physical or sexual abuse; modeling of aggression; media violence; negative attitude toward schooling; family transitions (death or divorce); parent criminality

Leads to Development of Maladaptive Behavioral Manifestations

defiance of adults; lack of school readiness; coercive interactive styles; aggression toward peers; lack of problem-solving skills

Produces Negative Short-Term Outcomes

truancy; peer and teacher rejection; low academic achievement; high number of school discipline referrals; large numbers of different schools attended; early involvement with drugs and alcohol; early age of first arrest (less than twelve years)

Leads to Negative, Destructive, Long-Term Outcomes

school failure and dropout; delinquency; drug and alcohol use; gang membership; violent acts; adult criminality; lifelong dependance on welfare system; higher death and injury rate

"Risk Path" Review

Think about the following questions as you review the "risk path":

- What practices or conditions in my school may make behavioral problems worse?

- Does the discipline process in my school help students accept and focus on restoring academic achievement, social relationships, and the learning environment?

Our Challenge: Responding to the Need

Having a clear understanding of the development of challenging behavior helps guide us toward a comprehensive response to the problem. Our challenge is to build the capacity to implement and sustain effective evidence-based interventions. Often discipline is meted out to students to "teach them a lesson" or to punish their actions. Research has shown that, while this may stop the behavior for a short time, chronic punishment coupled with school failure actually makes the problem worse.

The dominant response to challenging, violent, and potentially violent children and youth has been overwhelmingly characterized by the use of sanctions and punishing consequences. Typically, we wait until youth who are at risk fail school, drop out, and start offending before we seriously begin addressing the problems and challenges they present. These youths come to our attention through their contacts with public safety, law enforcement, juvenile court, and corrections officials. In far too many cases, especially with children and youths who are severely at risk, such delayed reactions are insufficient to effectively address the myriad problems posed by such behavior. Despite their exposure to multiple sanctions, including incarceration, many youths continue along the path to oftentimes violent adult criminality.

Generally, the warning signs of exposure to environmental risks are evident early on in the lives and school careers of children and youth. These warning signs vary substantially in terms of how well they predict or are associated with juvenile violence; all should be of serious concern, however. The more of these signs a student manifests, the greater the risk and the greater the urgency for appropriate intervention.

Punishment Itself Is Not a Solution—Punishing problem behaviors without a schoolwide positive support system results in increased:

Aggression • Vandalism • Truancy • Dropouts

(Mayer & Sulzer-Azaroff, 1990; Skiba, Peterson, & Williams, 1997)

Persistence of these risks over time is strongly associated with a host of negative developmental outcomes, including delinquency, school failure and dropout, drug and alcohol abuse, peer rejection, and sometimes violence (Loeber & Farrington, 1998). It is difficult and often impossible to reduce the environmental risk factors and conditions that produce these behaviors in children and youth who are at risk. But it is *very* important that the resulting behavioral risks be reduced, eliminated, or buffered by exposure to well-designed interventions (Vance, Fernandez, & Biber, 1998).

Keeping these students engaged with learning for as long as possible is one of the best things schools can do to prevent them from becoming involved with disruptive peer groups during school hours. Research on school discipline gives new insight into what is effective. While intuition may tell us that punishment or counseling approaches will work, other approaches actually show the most promise. The list in Figure 4 outlines best practices in school and classroom discipline. You will learn about many of these techniques as we progress through the book.

Figure 4

What Works in School and Classroom Discipline?

- School capacity to carry out interventions and keep them going

- Clear communication of behavior norms

- Positive school rules

- Consistent enforcement of behavioral expectations

- Positive reinforcement for expected behavior

- Communication of norms through schoolwide campaigns

- Effective classroom management

- Comprehensive social skills programs

- Instruction in techniques to improve problem-solving and impulse control skills

- Instruction in responsible decision making (limit setting)

- Positive behavioral support plans based on functional behavioral assessment

- Group behavior contingencies for expected behavior

- Instruction in self-management

- Differential reinforcement of expected behavior

- Token economies (class or schoolwide)

- Teacher approval or disapproval

(Gottfredson, 1997; Stage and Quiroz, 1997)

Now that we have reviewed effective practices in school and classroom discipline, we will demonstrate how to carry out some of these practices.

A Three-Tiered Model of Discipline Strategies

For interventions to work, prevention of problem behavior needs to be a priority. Effective schools approach the problem using a three-tiered model of discipline strategies. This model is based on extensive research about different child types and needs.

The three-tiered model depicted in Figure 5 defines the discipline challenge for schools as one that addresses the needs of three groups of students. The goal is to link each of these groups to a different level of discipline intervention—universal interventions (for all students), selected interventions (for some students), and targeted interventions (for a few students). One discipline strategy designed to fit all students will not work. Rather, schools need to use at least three (all, some, and few) different discipline efforts.

Best Behavior addresses schoolwide, classroom, and individual student interventions, as well as family collaboration, and it is one of the few programs that offers supports for *all* students in the school, *some* students with additional needs, and the *few* students who need the most intensive supports.

The model in Figure 5 shows why a single intervention or approach will not meet all the discipline and student support needs within a school. Our assumption is that one group of students (85 to 90 percent) will arrive at school already having learned important social and academic readiness skills. An important part of any schoolwide discipline and prevention program is to ensure that the skills of these students are embedded in the daily workings of the school. This can be accomplished through strategies aimed at *all* students. These interventions attempt to prevent problems before they start. The interventions must be efficient and low cost to deliver and can be provided to all students without prior individual assessment.

Interventions for all elementary and middle school students can take the form of direct social skills training in class; rules instruction for specific settings (e.g., playgrounds); positive

Figure 5

Three-Tiered Model of Schoolwide Discipline Strategies

3–5%
FEW
(Students Who Are High Risk)
Individual Interventions

7–10%
SOME
(Students Who Are At Risk)
Classroom and Small-Group Strategies

85–90%
ALL
(All Students)
Schoolwide Systems of Support

FEW	SOME	ALL
– Intensive academic support – Functional assessment – Individual behavior management plans – Parent training and collaboration – Multi-agency collaboration (wrap-around) – Alternative to suspension and expulsion – Community and service learning	– Intensive social skills teaching and support – Self-management programs – School-based adult mentors (checking in) – Increased academic support – Alternatives to out-of-school suspension	– Effective academic support – Social skills teaching – Effective classroom management – Teaching school behavior expectations – Active supervision and monitoring – Positive reinforcement for all students – Firm, fair, and corrective discipline – Data-based decision making

Adapted from Sprague, J., & Walker, H. (2000). Early identification and intervention for youth with antisocial and violent behavior. *Exceptional Children, 66*(3), 367–379.

reinforcement systems; consistent consequences; lessons to teach expected school behavior; or alcohol, tobacco, and other drug resistance programs. We believe that schools must closely monitor and teach *all* students, including those who currently are not engaging in problem behavior. These students must be "inoculated" against exposure to school, peer, and community risk factors and able to model positive social skills for their at-risk peers. The foundation of all effective schoolwide discipline efforts lies in attention to the universal training, adult modeling, monitoring, and reinforcement of expected social behavior to all students.

Not all students, however, respond as well to schoolwide approaches. Some students with chronic patterns of problem behavior require either more selected support or highly individualized and targeted support. The level and intensity of support is dictated by the level and complexity of the behavior problem. Interventions for some students (seven to ten percent) may require support from counselors, special educators, school psychologists, etc., and focus additional resources on the needs of small groups of students. Programs involving extra academic support, extra adult attention (school-based mentors), scheduling changes, self-management, and more frequent access to rewards can be used to improve the overall likelihood of school success and to reduce levels of problem behavior.

For the few students (three to five percent) who do not respond even to extra support, intensive, targeted intervention based on functional behavioral assessment procedures is required. These students will test the capacity of any school staff and will require intensive social skills training, individual behavior management plans, parent/caregiver training and collaboration, and multi-agency (wrap-around) service coordination.

Best Behavior focuses on each of the three tiers of behavior supports and on new and improved strategies for implementing them. A continuum of behavior support comprising three very different levels of intervention is needed. The intensity of the intervention must match the intensity of the problem behavior and the complexity of the context in which problem behavior occurs.

Interventions for all students focus on improving the overall level of appropriate behavior of most students but are not sufficient for some students and will have limited impact on the few students (three to five percent) with chronic patterns of problem behavior.

chapter 4

School Organization: Getting Started With *Best Behavior*

Chapter Objectives:

○ Outline the components of an effective schoolwide student support system

○ Identify, through the use of a self-assessment survey, the priorities for change in your school and classroom

○ Identify the top three or four priorities for improvement of school discipline systems in your school

From shrinking budgets to inconsistent discipline, teachers are faced with a variety of challenges, including:

- Doing more with less

- Coping with increased diversity (abilities, needs) in the classroom and school

- Managing students with severe problem behavior

- Keeping the good stuff going

- Achieving consistency among the adults

Use the following reflection to think about the challenges to effective school discipline that you may face.

> ## Reflection
>
> What are some challenges that you face in making your positive behavior support team work effectively?
>
> 1. _____
>
> 2. _____
>
> 3. _____

Foundations of an Effective Discipline Plan

One of the major problems in schools is that we have been unable to "fit" effective practices into the daily operations of our classrooms (Sugai & Horner, 1994). It's not that the practices we use are bad, but that we often don't attend to the processes necessary to get good programs off the ground and keep them going. In order to create an effective discipline plan, we need to build a strong foundation using the following principles:

- *Integrate the plan with school improvement.* School discipline goals should be an integral part of school improvement planning.

- *Make the principal an involved leader!* In our experience, no school discipline plan will be effective without active and substantive principal leadership.

- *Use standardized curriculum materials (for students and adults).* Simple, standardized materials will ease the effort of implementation, increase consistency, and provide an on-site resource.

- *Make sure most of the adults help implement the program.* It is essential that most, if not all, adults in the school teach, prompt, and recognize expected behavior.

- *Make sure that all students are involved (even the tough ones).* Universal intervention means just that: *all* students! Some students will need support beyond the universal strategies.

- *Make sure behavior/social skills are taught or reviewed about once per week.* Research from many perspectives indicates that learning social behavior is like exercise, we need to do it often and regularly to acquire and maintain essential skills and behaviors.

- *Include frequent, positive communication with families.* Some of us feel frustrated with a perceived lack of parent involvement, but we often do not take the time to implement simple, yet effective methods to work with parents as partners. Chapter 19 illustrates these methods.

Reflection

What are some of the "foundation pieces" that you see as important to effective behavior support in schools?

1. _____

2. _____

3. _____

Start by Completing a Needs Assessment

To begin your journey toward a more effective school program, we recommend that you complete the following needs assessment, the *Best Behavior* **Self-Assessment Survey**. While we strongly recommend that all adults in the school complete this assessment, you can also reflect on your own views about your school's status on each item. Once you have identified areas needing improvement, use the **Setting Goals** table that follows

the assessment to write goals and set concrete action steps. Your school behavior team will refer to these goals often and modify them as you gather key data regarding their effectiveness (e.g., office discipline referrals, rates of behavior on the playgound). We will cover data-based decision making later in the book.

Best Behavior Self-Assessment Survey

School Name: _____   Date: _____

Your Role (please choose one):

○ Administrator   ○ Teacher   ○ Classified   ○ Special Education Teacher

○ Related Service Provider   ○ Parent   ○ Student   ○ Other _____

Schoolwide Capacity

	In Place	Working on It	Not in Place	Targeted as Goal
1. A representative leadership team is formed to guide program implementation and evaluate its effectiveness.	○	○	○	○
2. The school administrator is an active member of the schoolwide behavior support team.	○	○	○	○
3. School personnel (80% or more) have committed to improving school discipline and safety by implementing, supporting, and agreeing to use positive behavioral support systems.	○	○	○	○
4. A needs assessment has been conducted to guide intervention selection.	○	○	○	○
5. An action plan with clear goals and objectives has been developed to improve school discipline.	○	○	○	○
6. Regular schoolwide behavior support team meetings are scheduled for training and planning.	○	○	○	○
7. Schoolwide behavior support has a budget for rewarding students (and staff), regular team meetings, teaching activities and materials, and data collection and analysis.	○	○	○	○

Schoolwide Behavioral Teaching and Intervention

	In Place	Working on It	Not in Place	Targeted as Goal
8. Three to five schoolwide behavior expectations have been defined (e.g., Be safe, respectful, responsible, etc.).	○	○	○	○
9. Positive behavior expectations have been defined for each school setting (e.g., what does "safe, respectful, responsible" look like in the cafeteria, gym, restrooms, etc.?).	○	○	○	○
10. Lesson plans have been developed for teaching all behavioral expectations in all school settings.	○	○	○	○

	In Place	Working on It	Not in Place	Targeted as Goal

11. Rules are posted and/or visible in all school settings (e.g., hallways, classrooms, cafeteria, gym, etc.)........... ○ ○ ○ ○

12. Staff has been trained to teach behavioral expectations..... ○ ○ ○ ○

13. Staff teaches behavioral expectations..................... ○ ○ ○ ○

14. Behavioral expectations for each rule are taught and reviewed at least ten times per year.................... ○ ○ ○ ○

15. Expected behaviors for each specific setting are taught in that setting at least one time a year.................... ○ ○ ○ ○

Recognizing and Rewarding Expected Behavior

16. A schoolwide system is defined for recognizing and rewarding appropriate, expected behavior............... ○ ○ ○ ○

17. Staff support and consistently use the schoolwide reward and recognition system in all settings. .... ○ ○ ○ ○

18. Staff attempt to have four positive interactions with students for every correctional or aversive interaction............ ○ ○ ○ ○

Dealing With Problem Behavior

19. Problem behaviors are clearly defined and explained to all students. .... ○ ○ ○ ○

20. Consequences for problem behaviors are clearly defined and explained to all students. .... ○ ○ ○ ○

21. Staff use consistent consequences for inappropriate behavior. ○ ○ ○ ○

22. Staff consistently correct and reteach students with problem behavior.................................... ○ ○ ○ ○

Data-Based Decision Making

23. Data are collected (discipline referrals, surveys) to guide decision making. .... ○ ○ ○ ○

24. Data are regularly summarized (e.g., at least monthly) by a discipline/behavior support team. .... ○ ○ ○ ○

	In Place	Working on It	Not in Place	Targeted as Goal
25. Staff receive regular (e.g., at least monthly) reports on key discipline outcomes (e.g., information about referrals, suspensions, etc.).	○	○	○	○
26. Intervention decisions and strategies are evaluated regularly (at least once per term) based on behavior data.	○	○	○	○

Classroom Management

27. The school has defined systems of classroom behavior management.	○	○	○	○
28. Curricula and instruction match student ability; students have high rates of academic success (75%+ correct).	○	○	○	○
29. Transitions within classrooms, between activities, and between settings are planned for, taught to students, well established, and orderly.	○	○	○	○

Individual Student Support

30. Teachers can easily get assistance with problem students in their classrooms.	○	○	○	○
31. Behavioral assessments are used to identify students with problem behavior.	○	○	○	○
32. A behavior support team attends promptly (within two school days) when a student exhibits chronic problem behavior.	○	○	○	○
33. Teachers are trained in, and use, effective methods to prevent behavioral escalation.	○	○	○	○
34. Teachers are trained in functional behavioral assessment and positive behavioral intervention for students with chronic problem behavior.	○	○	○	○

Family Support and Collaboration

35. Families are active participants in supporting schoolwide discipline systems.	○	○	○	○
36. The school supports good parenting practices by providing information and support to families.	○	○	○	○
37. The school has defined systems for regular, positive contacts with families.	○	○	○	○

Best Behavior • **chapter four**

	In Place	Working on It	Not in Place	Targeted as Goal
38. At least one parent is a member of the schoolwide positive discipline team	○	○	○	○
39. There is adequate staff on playgrounds, during recess and free time, and in other common areas to effectively supervise the number of students present.	○	○	○	○
40. A system of positive reinforcement is in place in all common area settings.	○	○	○	○
41. Recess, free time, playground, and/or common areas are easily observable (unobstructed views) from any given position in the area.	○	○	○	○
42. Supervisors make close contact with students in all recess, free time, playground, and/or common areas.	○	○	○	○
43. Playground, recess, or recreational equipment is safe.	○	○	○	○
44. Access to and from the playground, recess, or free-time areas is supervised.	○	○	○	○
45. Formal emergency or crisis procedures for students and staff on playgrounds, or in recess and other common areas, have been developed and are practiced at least twice a year.	○	○	○	○
46. Common area supervision staff have been trained in active supervision techniques and methods this year.	○	○	○	○
47. A system for addressing minor problem behavior in recess, playground, or common areas is in place and practiced by common-area supervision staff.	○	○	○	○
48. A system for addressing serious or major problem behavior in recess, playground, or common areas is in place and practiced by all common-area supervision staff.	○	○	○	○
49. Off-limits areas are clearly identified, taught to students and staff, and known by all.	○	○	○	○
50. All staff have received training in active supervision of common areas.	○	○	○	○

Setting Goals

Review the results of your self-assessment and identify the top three or four priorities for improvement of school discipline systems. List a clear goal statement, and then use the box on the right to set concrete action steps.

Improvement Goal	Action Steps
Goal 1	
Goal 2	
Goal 3	
Goal 4	

chapter 5

Defining Schoolwide Behavior Expectations

Chapter Objectives:

○ Discuss the importance of defining behavior expectations for your school

○ Outline features of effective schoolwide expectations

○ Define three to five positive behavioral expectations for your school

Developing school and classroom behavioral expectations is an important first step in building an effective positive discipline plan. Clearly stated expectations convey to students what teachers want. In addition, they tend to guide student behavior and strengthen teacher monitoring (Morgan & Jensen, 1988). It is critical to develop and secure agreement from all school adults on schoolwide behavior expectations before the start of school. We recommend that you teach these expectations on the first day of school and reinforce the expected behavior throughout the school year. (In Chapter 6, you will learn to develop lesson plans to teach the expectations and see a sample teaching schedule that can be adapted for your school.)

Developing and posting school behavior alone does not guarantee appropriate behavior (Greenwood, Hops, Delquadri, & Guild, 1974; Madsen, Becker, Thomas, Koser, & Plager, 1968). Teachers need to develop the rules, post them, teach them directly to students via role plays and practice, and provide frequent monitoring and positive feedback.

Why Do We Need Schoolwide Expectations?

Research has shown that teachers who are less effective at classroom management tend to rely on punishment (e.g., reprimands, criticism, and discussion) or removal from the classroom when students misbehave. A consistently reactive approach actually makes the problem behaviors worse, because the teacher gives most of his/her attention to inappropriate behaviors (Hagan, 1998). Another error is using many different approaches without clear definition for adults or students. If different teachers in the school use dramatically different approaches or have different expectations, students will be confused because expectations vary so much from class to class and setting to setting. For example, one teacher may allow students to be unsupervised while making the transition to recess, those students may run, push, or shove their classmates, while another teacher may actively supervise and monitor students as they exit the classroom.

Effective rule teaching or social skills programs have a number of common features and a goal of creating a culture of positive behavior in the school. It is important to address all forms of behavior in the school. For example, "be safe" (e.g., walk at all times), "be respectful" (e.g., follow adult directions), and "be responsible" (e.g., clean up after yourself) address the major classes of desirable behavior in schools (Walker, 1995).

School and classroom rules should state exactly what you expect from the students and target specific areas within the school setting. For example, students may be able to sit where they want at lunch but not in the auditorium. Figure 6 provides a "lesson in consistency." Take a moment to reflect on the schoolwide expectations in place now. Ask some of your colleagues what they think the expectations are. Is there consistency?

Figure 6

A Lesson in Consistency

To the best of your ability, list all of the school and classroom rules in place in your school and/or classroom. Do this by yourself and then share with your colleagues. If your rules and their rules don't match most of the time, you need to work on consistency!

School Rules

_____

_____

_____

_____

_____

_____

_____

Classroom Rules

_____

_____

_____

_____

_____

_____

_____

_____

What Do We Know About Effective Behavioral Expectations?

The following list presents the "big ideas" about developing and communicating schoolwide behavioral expectations.

What Do We Know About Effective Behavioral Expectations?

- They create a culture of consistency.

- They include all students for teaching.

- They use positively stated expectations.

- They target all forms of behavior (safe, respectful, responsible).

- They are known by all students and adults (ask them!).

Create a culture of consistency in the school. It is essential that all adults in the school, including paraprofessionals, parents, and noninstructional staff, know what is expected. Consistent expectations create a predictable and less stressful school environment and allow for effective correction of behavioral errors that teach students the "right way."

Include all students for teaching. It is necessary to include all students in the schoolwide plan. For typically developing students, communicating consistent expectations creates predictability, reduces the general level of disruption, and fosters a sense of belonging. If students know what is expected, it is easier for them to make good choices (e.g., comply with adult requests, get along with peers). Students with challenging behaviors will benefit even more from this consistent, clear environment, and teachers will have more opportunities to provide positive feedback and will react less to problematic behavior.

Use positively stated expectations. Research clearly indicates that students are much more likely to comply with "do" requests than "don't" requests. For example, "walk in the hallway" is more likely to promote compliance than "don't run in the hallway." The negatively stated expectation may even prompt running! If the expectation is stated positively, teachers are able to give positive feedback when they see the behavior they want

and more effectively correct a behavioral error. Stating expectations positively helps the adults attend to what they want, rather than what they don't want. Expectations should be stated in behavioral terms, that is, as what the behavior looks like. For example, "Students will walk in the hallway," not, "Students will behave in school" or "No running."

Target all forms of behavior. If we can help students be safe, responsible, and respectful, they are more likely to be successful in school and remain engaged in the schooling process. "Be safe" implies a feeling of social, emotional, and physical safety and creates a feeling of belonging. "Be respectful" relates to compliance to teacher requests and positive peer and adult relationships. "Be responsible" addresses school effort such as being ready for class, completing work, and keeping the school and classroom clean and orderly.

Known by all students and adults. It is common for schools to have a long list of "rules" in the student handbook and then assume that all students and adults "know" them. The rules in the school handbook (e.g., no weapons) are often required for administrative purposes to meet "due process" requirements for serious actions, such as suspension. Schools should also develop a simple list of expectations, such as "be safe, be respectful, and be responsible," and define what the behaviors look like in all settings of the school. You should be able ask any student or adult in the school about these expectations and get a consistent answer. If students can't state quickly what is expected, they won't know what to do in the moment. If teachers are not clear about what they want students to do, then they are more likely to punitively correct students, thus setting up noncompliance or behavioral escalation. If the adults in the school agree upon and can state all specific behavior expectations, minor inappropriate behaviors diminish significantly (Sprague et al., 2001).

Developing School Rules

We recommend that you take some time to develop school rules and behavior expectations that are unique to your school. This will work best if you work in a team representing all stakeholders in your school (see Chapters 2 and 4). Figures 7–9 provide sample "behavioral expectations matrices" for an elementary, middle, and high school. You may need to adapt this

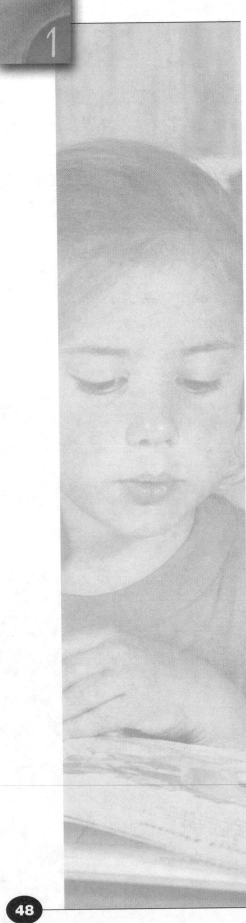

format, depending on the age level of your students and local norms and values about expected behavior. The following steps are a guideline:

1. Review the **Defining Schoolwide Expectations Worksheet** at the end of this chapter.

2. Decide on three to four umbrella rules (e.g., be safe, be responsible, be respectful).

3. Make a list of common areas in your school.

4. Define the expectations and complete the matrix for each setting.

5. When the matrix is completed, share with all of the adults in the school (and with students as appropriate) and obtain agreement regarding the expectations.

Some of you may be wondering, "Does this really work?" Researchers have demonstrated that these types of programs, when paired with monitoring and a system of positive reinforcement, can reduce problem behavior and improve school climate (Sprague et al., 2001; Taylor-Greene et al., 1997).

Figure 7

Elementary School Rules and Behavioral Expectations for Common Areas Matrix

Common Area	Be Safe	Be Respectful	Be Responsible
All Common Areas	• Walk facing forward. • Keep hands, feet and objects to self. • Get adult help for accidents and spills. • Use all equipment and materials appropriately.	• Use kind words and actions. • Wait for your turn. • Clean up after self. • Follow adult directions.	• Follow school rules. • Remind others to follow school rules. • Take proper care of all personal belongings and school equipment. • Be honest.
Cafeteria	• Keep all food to self. • Sit with feet on floor, bottom on bench, and facing table.	• Allow anyone to sit next to you. • Use quiet voices.	• Raise hand and wait to be excused. • Get all utensils, milk, etc., when first going through the line.
Playground/Recess	• Walk to and from the playground. • Stay within boundaries. • Be aware of activities/games around you.	• Play fairly. • Include everyone.	• Use hall/bathroom pass for leaving the area.
Passing Areas, Halls, Breezeways, Sidewalks	• Stay to the right. • Allow others to pass.	• Hold the door open for the person behind you. • Use quiet voices.	• Stay on sidewalks.
Bathrooms	• Keep feet on floor. • Keep water in sink. • Wash hands. • Put towels in garbage can.	• Knock on stall door. • Give people privacy. • Use quiet voices.	• Flush toilet after use. • Return to room promptly. • Use a bathroom pass.
Arrival and Dismissal Areas	• Use bike lane. • Use sidewalks and crosswalks. • Wait in designated areas.	• (See **All Common Areas**)	• Arrive on time. • Leave on time. • Get teacher permission to use the classroom phone.
Media/Gym	• (See **All Common Areas**)	• Use quiet voices.	• Use hall pass for leaving the area.
Special Events and Assemblies	• Wait for arrival and dismissal signal.	• Use audience manners. • Sit on bottom.	• (See **All Common Areas**)

Middle School Rules and Behavioral Expectations for Common Areas Matrix

Common Area	Be Safe	Be Responsible	Be Respectful
Cafeteria	• Walk at all times. • Eat only your own food.	• Wait in line patiently. • All food and drink stays in cafeteria. • Place recyclables in proper containers.	• Use good manners. • Clean up your area.
Gym	• Sit properly in bleachers/chairs. • Use equipment properly. • No food, drink, or gum.	• Show good sportsmanship. • Return equipment to designated area.	• Be a team player, encourage others. • Use home court.
Assemblies/Special Events	• Sit quietly during presentation. • Wait for dismissal instructions.	• Focus on presentation.	• Listen responsibly. • Applaud appropriately.
Media Center	• Keep hands and feet to self. • Use chairs and tables appropriately.	• Return materials to proper places on time. • Use Internet appropriately, print only what's needed. • No food, drink, or gum.	• Use kind words and actions. • Respect property—yours and others'.
Hallways	• Walk at all times. • Keep hands and feet to self. • Move to class on time.	• No food, drink, or gum. • Use drinking fountains appropriately.	• Use kind words and actions. • Respect property—yours and others'.
Office/SRC	• Keep hands and feet to self. • Use chairs and tables appropriately.	• State your purpose politely. • Obtain permission to use phone. • No food, drink, or gum.	• Use kind words and actions. • Keep hands and feet to yourself.
Bathrooms	• Keep water in sink. • Wash hands. • Put towels in garbage.	• Flush toilets. • Inform adults of vandalism.	• Give people privacy. • Respect property—yours and others'.
Bicycles/Walkers	• Walk and ride bikes safely. • Wear helmets. • Secure bicycles. • No loitering.	• Touch others' property only with permission. • Pick up litter.	• Use kind words and actions. • Respect property—yours and others'.
Bus Area	• Do not block front doors. • Stay behind yellow line.	• Wait in line patiently. • No gum. • Pick up litter.	• Use kind words and actions. • Keep hands and feet to yourself.

Figure 9

High School Rules and Behavioral Expectations for Common Areas Matrix

Common Area	Be Safe	Be Responsible	Be Respectful
Classroom	• Keep hands and feet to self. • Ask permission to leave assigned areas. • Follow directions and safety procedures. • Keep walkways clear.	• Treat others' property with respect. • Follow directions and classroom assignments. • Actively listen to designated speaker. • Use appropriate voice and words.	• Be prepared and on time. • Stay on task. • Resolve attendance issues before class. • Sign in/sign out. • Clean up after self.
All Common Areas	• Follow adult directions the first time given.		
Bus Area	• Keep hands and feet to self. • When buses are present, remain on sidewalk. • Walk at all times.	• Treat others and property with respect. • Use appropriate voice and language. • No harassment.	• Pick up your trash. • Remind others to follow rules.
Eating Areas	• Keep hands and feet to self. • Walk at all times. • Keep walkways clear.	• Treat others and property with respect. • Use appropriate voice and language.	• Clean up after self. • Remind others to follow rules.
Assembly	• Keep hands and feet to self. • Enter and exit in an orderly fashion. • Keep walkways clear.	• Be attentive. • Listen with an open mind. • Remove hats when requested. • Applaud appropriately.	• Sit quietly. • Remind others to follow rules.
Hallway	• Keep hands and feet to self. • Keep walkways clear. • Walk at all times.	• Treat others and property with respect. • Use appropriate voice and language.	• Pick up your trash. • Inform staff of spills and wait for help.

Defining Schoolwide Expectations Worksheet

Name of School: _____

Common Area	Be Safe	Be Responsible	Be Respectful

chapter 6

Teaching Schoolwide Behavior Expectations

Chapter Objectives:

○ Describe methods for teaching and encouraging desired behavior

○ Develop a school lesson plan

○ Set a schedule to teach and review expected behavior lessons

Positive school behavioral expectations have the following features:

- Expectations are positively stated.

- Expectations are posted: in hallways, classrooms, in the school handbook, on agenda planners, etc.

- Expectations are taught directly to students with formal lessons.

- Expectations are taught and reviewed at least 10–20 times per year.

- To maximize effectiveness, a system of positive reinforcement and recognition—at all times, by all adults—for following the expectations is in place throughout the building.

Once faculty and staff have defined schoolwide expectations, these must be taught directly to students. In the past, students were taught how to behave well at home, but now more and more students arrive at the schoolhouse door without the basic social skills needed for school success. They may have learned that it is appropriate to hit, push, or call names to resolve a conflict. They may not have learned to comply with reasonable adult requests. To counter these behavior patterns, students must be directly taught appropriate school behavior and given ample opportunity to practice. We cannot assume that students already know what is expected in the school setting.

Teach Expected Behaviors Just Like Other Subjects

Strategies for teaching and managing social behavior are the same as strategies used to teach reading, math, physics, music, etc. Social and academic management strategies must be integrated within and across the curricula. In each class-room and in every area of the school, it is important to do the following:

1. Target specific times to teach the expectations. This may be done the first few days of school. Teachers may decide to have teaching stations (e.g., cafeteria, playground, hallway, and bathroom) and rotate all students through each station. Students could carry a "passport"; upon completion of each station, students receive a stamp and go on to the next station. Middle and high schools may decide to have "staggered" starting days for each grade level. Each grade level would spend one entire day learning about each teaching station. A school may decide to make a video of expectations and show it during a schoolwide assembly.

2. Intervene with students, using the language of the lessons. For example if a student is running in the hall, say: *"What is the rule about all hallways? Please go back and walk."*

3. Watch for students who are using the expected behaviors, and give them positive feedback.

4. Review and recall expected behaviors regularly.

5. Use the language of behavior expectations in content lessons such as history or social studies, or when reading stories to your students.

6. Model the expected behaviors in all of your interactions with students and adults.

Social skills instruction increases in intensity, specialization, and individualization as problems become more chronic. Just like academic skills, it is important to teach behavior in the same manner as any academic subject. Teaching expectations involves demonstrating and modeling, rehearsal and guided practice, corrective feedback and regular reviews. To ensure that students clearly understand the expectations, give examples and nonexamples of what they mean. For the expectation, "When the teacher asks you to do something, do it right away," students should be shown how to do it the right way (quickly) as well as examples of the wrong way (too slow, complaining). Figure 10 presents the "big ideas" about teaching social behaviors.

Figure 10

Teach Social Behavior Like Academic Skills

- Teach through multiple examples.

- Teach where the problems are occurring.

- Give frequent practice opportunities.

- Provide useful corrections.

- Provide positive feedback.

- Monitor for success.

Figure 11 presents the components of a model school expectations lesson plan and Figure 12 provides a sample lesson plan.

Figure 11

School Expectations: Lesson Plan Components

- What do we expect the student to do?

  —Teach the expected behaviors.

  —Tell why it is important.

  —Give positive and negative examples.

  —Provide opportunities for practice.

- Prevent problems from occurring.

  —Actively supervise.

  —Provide reminders of expected behavior before they occur.

  —Give positive feedback for expected behavior.

  —Provide corrections for problem behavior.

  —Review behavioral expectations.

  —Measure for success.

Develop a School Lesson Plan

Please take a moment to practice developing a school expectations lesson plan. Use the blank **Expected Behavior Lesson Plan** form; select one of your school expectations (from Chapter 5), and develop a lesson plan. Work with your team members to develop a complete lesson using the sample in Figure 12, Expected Behavior Lesson Plan. We recommend that you practice teaching your lesson by doing a role play.

Figure 12

Expected Behavior Lesson Plan (sample)

The Topic/Rule: Be respectful

What do we expect the student to do?

1. Speak respectfully to adults and peers.
2. Use respectful words to resolve conflicts.
3. Keep hands and feet to self in common areas.

How will we teach the expected behavior?

Tell why following the rule is important: It is important to be respectful to your peers and adults in the school. Using words or actions to harass, tease, or bully another person is inappropriate and can hurt others physically or emotionally. Negative interactions in the school interfere with learning and can cause problems at school and in the community.

List examples and nonexamples of the expected behaviors (at least three each): Ask students to identify examples and nonexamples of each part of the rule. Ask them to identify both and tell why it is a good or bad example of expected behavior. These are examples you might use:

- A positive example: Joe bumped into Mary in the hallway and her books fell to the ground. She was upset because she would be late to class and started to call him names. Joe recognized that he was not paying attention and decided to apologize and help Mary pick up her books. His teacher gave him a positive referral, and Mary thanked him for resolving the problem with respect.

- A nonexample: Joe bumped into Mary in the hallway and her books fell to the ground. She was upset because she would be late to class and called Joe a "jerk." Joe got angry and told Mary she was ugly and stupid. He walked away, and Mary was late for class. Mary was mad and began to spread untrue rumors about Joe to her friends.

Teachers should prompt students to (a) identify the problem, (b) think of one or more respectful solutions to the problem, (c) choose one of the solutions, (d) carry it out, and (e) evaluate the solution.

Provide opportunities to practice and build fluency:

1. Set aside a few minutes at the beginning of each period to practice the rule.
2. As the teacher models, have individual students demonstrate examples and nonexamples of following the rule (role play).
3. Tell students about the consequences for following and not following the rules.

57

Expected Behavior Lesson Plan

The Topic/Rule: _____

What do we expect the student to do?

How will we teach the expected behavior?

Tell why following the rule is important:

List examples and nonexamples of the expected behaviors (at least three each):

Provide opportunities to practice and build fluency:

Schedule Lesson Times

Once your sample lesson plans are developed, it is critical to set a schedule for teaching the lessons. It is common to review or teach expected behavior at the beginning of the year, but expected behavior will only be maintained when the lessons are reviewed regularly. We recommend that a lesson or other activity regarding expected behavior be provided about weekly. Figure 13 provides a sample year-long lesson teaching schedule. Take some time to review this plan, and then set a time to schedule behavior teaching across the school year.

Figure 13

Sample Behavior Expectations Lesson Schedule

Week 1 (Sept 5)
Basic Behavior Expectations, Classroom, Playground, Bus, Library, Zero Tolerance, and Substitute Teacher

Week 2 (Sept 11)
Repeat of Week 1

Week 3 (Sept 18)
Repeat of Weeks 1 & 2

Week 4 (Sept 25)
All Common Areas

Week 5 (Oct 2)
Cafeteria

Week 6 (Oct 9)
No lessons/3-day week

Week 7 (Oct 16)
Playground

Week 8 (Oct 23)
Passing Areas

Week 9 (Oct 30)
Bathrooms

Week 10 (Nov 6)
No lessons/ 3-day week

Week 11 (Nov 13)
Arrival and Dismissal

Week 12 (Nov 20)
No lessons/conferences and no school

Week 13 (Nov 27)
Bus Safety

Week 14 (Dec 4)
Common Instructional Areas and Library

Week 15 (Dec 11)
Special Events and Assemblies

Winter Break (Dec 18)

Week 16 (Jan 2)
Review Basic Behavior Expectations, Classroom, Playground, Bus, Library, Zero Tolerance, and Substitute Teacher

Week 17 (Jan 8)
Repeat of Week 1

Week 18 (Jan 16)
Repeat of Weeks 1 & 2

Week 19 (Jan 22)
All Common Areas

Week 20 (Jan 30)
Cafeteria

Week 21 (Feb 5)
Playground

Week 22 (Feb 12)
Passing Areas

Week 23 (Feb 19)
No lessons/3-day week

Week 24 (Feb 26)
Bathrooms

Week 25 (Mar 5)
Arrival and Dismissal

Week 26 (Mar 12)
Bus Safety

Week 27 (Mar 19)
Common Instructional Areas and Library

Spring Break (Mar 26)

Week 28 (Apr 2)
Special Events and Assemblies

Week 29 (Apr 9)
Restricted Areas

Week 30 (Apr 16)
Zero-Tolerance Behaviors

Week 31 (Apr 23)
No lessons/conferences

Week 32 (Apr 30)
Lesson Review

Weeks 33–36
Lesson Review

chapter 7

Schoolwide Recognition and Reward Systems: Creating a Positive School Culture

Chapter Objectives:

○ Discuss issues regarding positive reinforcement

○ Plan to implement a schoolwide recognition and reward system

○ Discuss how to increase consistency among the adults in the school

○ Develop the recognition and reward plan

It is common to focus on punishing or stopping disruptive behavior, but students with challenging behaviors will not make meaningful educational progress unless they are taught skills that increase their ability to function successfully in the school. Walker et al. (1996) showed that posting rules alone had no effect on student misbehavior, but when teachers were instructed to teach school rules, "catch students being good," and ignore minor inappropriate behaviors, problem behaviors dropped dramatically.

To begin, it is important to discuss issues and concerns regarding the use of positive reinforcement methods in schools. The following reflection presents some issues that others have raised regarding use of positive reinforcement (Webster-Stratton & Herbert, 1994). Please take a moment to think about each of these issues and identify your own opinions and values regarding these methods. You might also consider discussing them with your colleagues.

Reflection

What You Always Wanted to Know About Praise and Rewards

1. ***Shouldn't children at this age already know what is expected of them and how to behave?***
   Behavior that is acknowledged is more likely to occur again. Behavior that is ignored is less likely to be repeated. No good behavior should be taken for granted or it may decline, regardless of the student's age.

2. ***Praising feels unnatural. Won't kids think that it is phony?***
   If you are not used to praising, it will feel unnatural at first. But the more you praise, the more natural it will feel. If you praise good behavior that truly has happened, there is nothing phony about it. Students who get praise will tend to praise others too, so praise won't seem phony to them.

3. ***Isn't praise manipulative and coercive?***
   The purpose of praise is to reinforce and increase positive behavior with the student's knowledge. Praise helps clearly describe expectations so that students can successfully meet them. Helping children succeed is a positive thing to do!

4. ***Isn't giving a reward like bribing students to do what you want them to do?***
   A bribe attempts to influence or persuade someone to produce a desired behavior that hasn't yet happened, whereas a reward reinforces a desired behavior that has already happened. A reward is given after the behavior occurs.

5. ***Won't students come to depend on tangible rewards? Don't extrinsic rewards decrease intrinsic motivation?***
   Tangible rewards should be accompanied by social rewards. When a message that recognizes a student's efforts as being responsible for success is given with a reward, internal motivation will actually be strengthened.

6. ***Shouldn't rewards be saved for special achievements?***
   This gives students the message that everyday behaviors and efforts don't count. Small steps on the way to achievement (such as homework completion) also need to be recognized and rewarded.

7. ***Where will I get enough money to supply all these rewards?***
   Tangible rewards need not be too expensive. As students learn the desired behavior, the tangible rewards can gradually be faded out. Rewards can be privileges too, such as being able to go to lunch first or getting extra computer time.

8. ***Do students in middle school and high school still need rewards?***
   People of all ages, including adults, need to be recognized and rewarded for their efforts. Students of all ages do need recognition, praise, and rewards, particularly during the difficult transition to adolescence.

Adapted by J.C. Rusby from Webster-Stratton, C., & Herbert M. (1994). *Troubled families—Problem children.* New York: John Wiley & Sons.

Implementing a Consistent Schoolwide Recognition System

The biggest influence on the success of recognition systems is consistency among the adults in the school. While at first it seems paradoxical, we have found that the more you pay attention to behaviors (good or bad), the more you will get those behaviors. For example, if students are misbehaving and you constantly reprimand them, they may actually misbehave more. It is better to "catch" the students being safe, responsible, and/or respectful. You will see more of the behavior you want.

Features of Schoolwide Recognition Systems

The following list outlines the features of effective schoolwide recognition systems. The reinforcement system should be implemented across the entire school. All students in the school should have access to positive feedback, even those who "challenge" the system.

Implementing a Schoolwide Reward and Recognition System

- Design the system for all students.
- Give public recognition to model for other students.
- Use recognition and rewards that students want.
- Recognize teachers as well!
- Increase recognition before difficult times.
- Reteach behaviors if things don't go well.

Recognition should be made public. Research has shown that public display and delivery of recognition has a powerful modeling effect. When students see their peers get recognized for good behavior, they will be motivated to display the same behaviors. As students get older, public recognition may not work for some students who prefer private feedback about their behavior. We have found, however, that students really enjoy it when their teacher gets recognized.

Use recognition that is meaningful to students (e.g., social, tangible, or activity). Good ways to find out what students want include asking them to participate in development of the recognition program and observing their behavior when recognitions are delivered. If they are not excited or fail to respond to the recognition, it may be time to choose others. Variety in recognitions also increases their value.

Recognize teachers as well. Teachers can also benefit from recognition and "surprises" for their hard work and participation in the program.

Increase reinforcement before difficult times. There are predictable times of the year (e.g., before holidays, vacations, or tests) when students are more likely to be disruptive. It is recommended that rule reteaching "boosters" and increased recognition and monitoring be provided during these times.

Reteach behaviors if things don't go well. Even the best systems will not be perfect. As problem spots are noted, use rule teaching "boosters" and increased positive reinforcement and monitoring.

The Reinforcement and Recognition Plan for "Lucky Middle School"

Figure 14 provides an example of a school that uses rich and varied reinforcement strategies. Please review the plan from the fictional Lucky Middle School and use the reflection that follows it to ponder the implications for your school.

Figure 14

Provide Positive Feedback—Recognize and Reward Expected Behavior: The Plan for Lucky Middle School

Reward System	Individual Students	Whole Class	School-wide	Parents	Teachers/ Staff
1. Good-news referral (student goes to the office to be recognized)	X				X
2. Good-news calls to home	X			X	
3. Teacher-delivered good behavior tokens	X	X			
4. Positive teacher notes in student planner	X			X	
5. Student-delivered good behavior tokens	X				
6. Value coupons obtained from local businesses (e.g.,two-for-one movie ticket)	X			X	X
7. Activity coupons (e.g., extra recess)	X	X	X		X
8. Good behavior activities or trips	X	X	X		
9. Media recognition (e.g., loudspeaker, newsletters, newspaper)	X				
10. Postcards or self-management checklists sent home (see Chapter 18)	X	X	X	X	X

Reflection

The Lucky Middle School Program

- Which features of the Lucky Middle School plan do you like?

- Which features could you use in your school?

- What systems do you have in your school or classroom now?

Develop Your Reward and Recognition Plan

Students may be motivated by the following consequences for their behavior: (1) adult attention, (2) peer attention, (3) avoidance of an activity or task, and (4) something tangible. An efficient and effective way to get their needs met is to misbehave. When misbehavior occurs, the teachers (or peers) respond to it quickly. For example, if a student has been working quietly, no one may give attention to her. But, if she misbehaves (e.g., whines, screams, throws objects), she will get attention immediately. She gets what she needs and the acting-out behavior is reinforced. While some students will need a greater amount of attention, we have found that we need to maintain at least a four-to-one ratio of positive to negative interactions with every student.

Teachers should also recognize students for ignoring the disruptive behavior of others and for displaying appropriate behavior. Chapter 13 provides instruction on how to teach this important skill.

Now that we have covered the basics of developing recognition systems, you will have an opportunity to develop a system for use in your school or classroom (see Figure 15). A recognition system using tokens (e.g., tickets, buttons) is a simple way of creating a consistent recognition system. When used in combination with reduced attention for minor problems and correcting behavioral errors, this type of system is effective in reducing challenging behavior.

Feel free to use the reproducible sample school tokens at the end of this chapter or design your own.

Figure 15

Checklist of Essential Components of a School-wide Recognition System

Give a clear statement of the expected behavior for each item (use the behavior expectations you developed in Chapter 5). Then answer the following questions:

Be Safe • Be Respectful • Be Responsible

○ Who will be involved (e.g., teachers, staff, administrator, volunteers, others)?

○ How and when will tokens be distributed?

○ Where will the tokens be turned in?

○ What "backup" incentives will be used?

○ How and where will you obtain backup rewards?

○ When and where will drawings for backup incentives occur?

○ Who will conduct the drawings?

○ When will you review if the system is working?

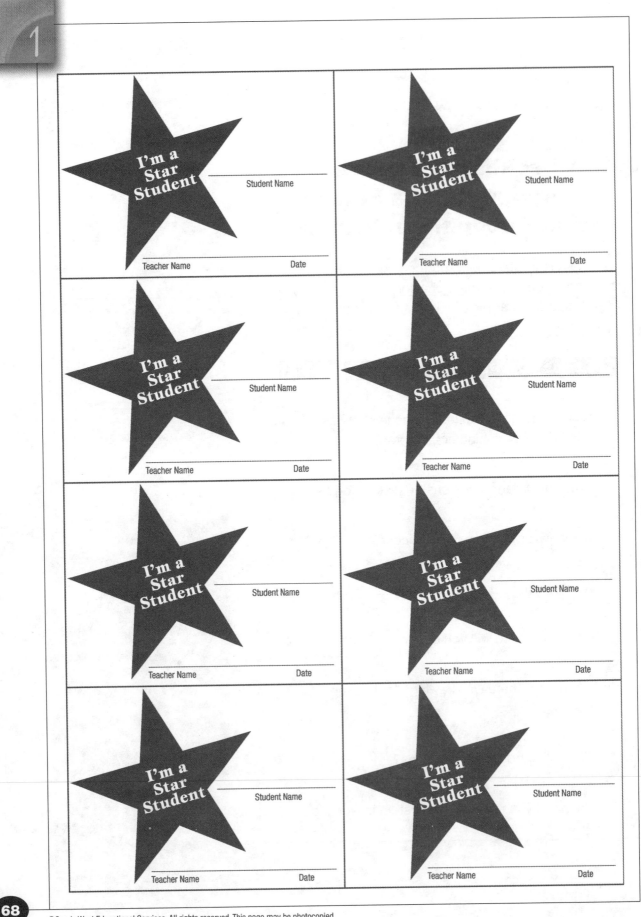

I'm a
Star
Student

Student Name

Teacher Name   Date

I'm a
Star
Student

Student Name

Teacher Name   Date

I'm a
Star
Student

Student Name

Teacher Name   Date

I'm a
Star
Student

Student Name

Teacher Name   Date

I'm a
Star
Student

Student Name

Teacher Name   Date

I'm a
Star
Student

Student Name

Teacher Name   Date

I'm a
Star
Student

Student Name

Teacher Name   Date

I'm a
Star
Student

Student Name

Teacher Name   Date

Student Name	Points Earned

For Being...

Teacher	Date

Student Name	Points Earned

For Being...

Teacher	Date

Student Name	Points Earned

For Being...

Teacher	Date

Student Name	Points Earned

For Being...

Teacher	Date

Student Name	Points Earned

For Being...

Teacher	Date

Student Name	Points Earned

For Being...

Teacher	Date

Student Name	Points Earned

For Being...

Teacher	Date

Student Name	Points Earned

For Being...

Teacher	Date

69

chapter seven • Best Behavior

chapter 8

Active Supervision of Common Areas

Chapter Objectives:

- Define active supervision
- Describe active supervision techniques
- Develop a reward plan for one area of your school

"Active supervision" is a term applied to a multi-element method of student behavior support and management. Active supervision methods work well in the following conditions: (1) large area, (2) high-census (lots of students), (3) lightly staffed (one or two adults for every 80 + students), and (4) unstructured activity (student-directed) in an area such as a playground, cafeteria, hallway, etc. Active supervision techniques also work very well in classrooms and other medium- to small-group activities or areas.

Common Area Rules and Behavioral Expectations

It is important to emphasize that simply maintaining an adult presence in common areas and merely attending to select inappropriate behaviors is an insufficient and

ineffective intervention practice. Supervisors need to: (1) help develop and know the rules, (2) be able to effectively and efficiently teach the rules, (3) be able to effectively and efficiently enforce the rules, and (4) provide frequent monitoring and positive feedback.

Features of Active Supervision

There are seven major features in a comprehensive active supervision program. The first three features are usually described as core active supervision techniques. Features four, five, and six are behavior support practices utilizing schoolwide positive behavior support strategies and efficient and effective correction approaches. Feature seven is a team-based element designed to promote data-based decision making and consistent application and delivery of the first six features on a regular, ongoing basis. Table 1 on the next page outlines the features of active supervision.

Movement

Why is movement important? There are many reasons, but the most important in terms of supervision are: (1) greater visibility of, and direct observation by, the supervisor across more students, areas, and activities; (2) increased rate of proximity to more students; (3) increased opportunity for supervisor/student contact; (4) increased opportunity for positive reinforcement of appropriate behavior; and (5) increased likelihood of encountering covert inappropriate behaviors such as bullying and harassment.

What constitutes effective movement? Movement should encompass three main practices in order to be effective and efficient. First, movement should be constant. Constant movement tends to give students the impression that you're everywhere at once. Constant movement increases the opportunity to have positive contacts with more students and to stay in close proximity for behavior management and support. Movement should be planned, constant, and deliberate unless attention or action is required at one specific location.

Second, movement patterns should be randomized and unpredictable. If possible, supervisor movements should follow no

Table 1

Features of Active Supervision

	Feature	Elements/Components
1.	Movement	a. Constant b. Randomized c. Targets known problem areas
2.	Scanning	a. Constant b. Targets both appropriate and inappropriate behaviors c. Targets known problem areas d. Uses both visual and aural cues e. Increases opportunities for positive contact
3.	Positive Contact	a. Friendly, helpful, open demeanor b. Proactive, noncontingent c. High rate of delivery
4.	Positive Reinforcement	a. Immediate b. Contingent on behavior c. Consistent (with behavior and across staff) d. High rate
5.	Instructional Responses	a. Immediate b. Contingent on behavior c. Nonargumentative, noncritical d. Specific to behavior e. Systematic: correction, model, lead, test, and retest f. Consistent (with behavior and across staff)
6.	Immediate and Contingent Delivery of Aversive Consequences (Punishers)	a. Neutral, businesslike demeanor b. Nonargumentative, noncritical c. Consistent (with behavior and across staff) d. Fair, nonarbitrary
7.	Team-Directed, Data-Based Decision Making and Intervention Implementation	a. Administrative buy-in and support b. Regular weekly meetings c. Intervention and behavior data collection and analysis d. Interstaff participation and communication e. Part of a schoolwide behavior support program

regular or set pattern. Students become used to routines, and opportunities for inappropriate behavior may be established and exploited by students when exposed to a predictable, set supervisory routine. Although it is necessary for movements to have a plan that establishes close proximity to all students, areas, and activities being supervised, the patterns of movement should be varied from period to period and day to day.

Finally, movement strategies should target known problem areas, activities, and individuals at as high a rate as practicable.

What are the benefits of effective movement strategies? Engaging in effective movement techniques increases: (a) opportunities for supervisor attention to both appropriate and inappropriate behaviors, (b) opportunities for high rates of positive to negative or corrective interactions with students, and (c) opportunities for supervisors to encounter and intervene in covert inappropriate behavior.

Scanning

Common areas such as hallways, cafeterias, playgrounds, and free-time areas are typically high-census in terms of students-to-adult ratio, large and irregular in shape, and difficult for a supervisor to effectively cover. As we have discussed, high rates of movement can greatly increase supervisor effectiveness in these areas. But what about the more distant, obscure, or hidden areas outside the immediate presence of the supervisor as he or she moves about? The mastery and use of scanning techniques can give the supervisor an effective "long-range" tool.

Too often we tend to observe only those things close at hand—especially in high-activity, high-census situations. It is natural for supervisors to focus on activities or individuals that are close by. Developing the ability to systematically scan more distant parts of an area and recognize signs or sounds that may indicate problem behavior is invaluable to effective common-area supervision. Some of the more useful scanning methods and techniques:

- Maintain a constant visual movement whether standing, walking, or talking. Shift your field of view with attention to visual indicators that target behaviors. This type of scanning practice increases the ability to make more noncontingent positive contact, and it expands the supervisor's area of proximity by making eye contact with students outside the supervisor's immediate physical area. This practice also increases the opportunity for positive visual contact and reinforcement: Supervisors should smile and wave to students who are engaged in expected, appropriate behaviors outside their immediate physical area.

- Train yourself to look at the students' *behavior(s)*, not just their games, their clothes, their hair, etc. People tend to look at familiar individuals without attention to subtle contextual, physical, or behavior clues that may be signs of distress.

- Train yourself to look at the "big picture"—not just one student or activity but as much activity as possible. People who watch students play often find themselves watching the game, instead of attending to the exhibited behaviors.

- Identify and attend to behaviors that are typically associated with target behaviors, such as games breaking up for no apparent reason; students frowning and gesturing to others, perhaps angrily; students seemingly shrinking back from a peer or peers; quick, violent movements for unapparent reasons; someone running away from a peer or peers outside of any apparent game; scared looks; someone making a fist or obscene gesture; etc.

- Train yourself to listen for behavior. Physical disposition is not always a good indicator of what may be happening. There are many attendant aural cues that a target behavior may be taking place at a distance, such as angry or whining and plaintive tones of voice, arguing, panicked voices, and bossy and authoritative voices or commands. Try to keep eyes in one direction and ears in another while scanning.

- Train yourself to focus on as many different areas as you can. Start small and work to increase your field of awareness.

- Train yourself to recognize potential trouble spots and scan them often. For example, tetherball is often a source of arguing, typically leading to verbal and sometimes physical aggression. The supervisors need

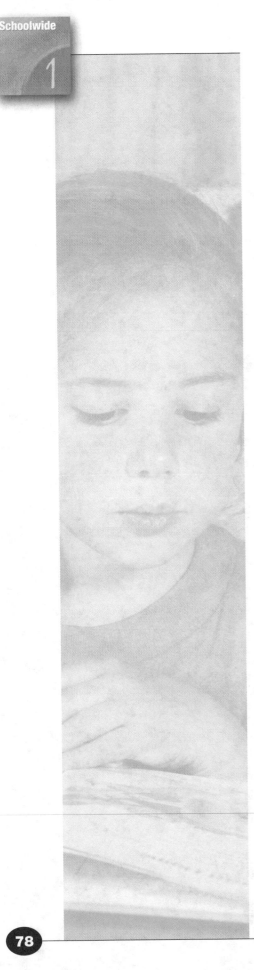

to move around to all areas but keep an eye on the tetherball game for signs that something is interfering with the game (e.g., the game has stopped, and someone is holding the ball and keeping it away from others).

- Train yourself to recognize situations that may precede problem behavior (see Chapter 14: Responding to Escalating Behavior and Verbal Harassment). As seen in the previous example, problem behaviors such as aggression are typically preceded by arguing, rough play, high states of arousal, or unsportsmanlike conduct and over-competitiveness. Supervisors who recognize these precursor behaviors and take immediate action can often stop the behaviors before they escalate.

- Maximize both movement and scanning opportunities by minimizing time spent dealing with problem behaviors. Use the "Two-Minute Rule." If you can't solve a problem or correct a behavior in two minutes or less, then refer the problem to the office (depending on severity) or some other prearranged place. If the problem is not severe and processing with the student or students can wait, defer lengthy intervention until after the recess ends and students are back in class or other structured activities. Then, at a later time, the supervisor can finish correcting the student or students in private and without interfering with supervision during recess. When identified, solve or correct problems quickly, fairly, consistently and as privately as possible and move on.

Positive Contact

Positive contacts between school staff and students should encompass a few specific elements. In general, staff should actively project a friendly, helpful, open demeanor, especially when in close proximity to students who are appropriately engaged and exhibiting expected behavior. Supervisors and school staff should cultivate a "personal touch" when in contact with students. This personal touch should establish the staff member's role as a caring member of the school community, fostering trust and respect with the students. In addition, staff should pay attention to maintaining their authoritative role in the school community. Positive contact should be proactive. Staff should actively pursue and engineer opportunities for positive contact with students. Positive contacts establish attention for appropriate behaviors, increasing the likelihood that they will occur while decreasing the incidence of inappropriate behaviors.

Positive contacts are noncontingent rather than prompted by, or based on, a specific student behavior—as long as the behavior at the time is not inappropriate. Avoid inadvertently rewarding inappropriate behavior if at all possible.

Staff should strive to sustain a high rate of positive contact delivery. It is recommended that staff maintain at least a four- or five-to-one ratio of positive to negative contacts. Positive contacts can provide opportunities to precorrect students concerning appropriate versus inappropriate behavior. Deliberately engineering positive contact with those students who are at risk or high risk in terms of problem behavior may allow the supervisor to precorrect those students before they have a chance to misbehave.

Positive Reinforcement

In contrast to positive contact, positive reinforcement is contingent upon specific student behavior. That is, the student must demonstrate a specific appropriate behavior that has been targeted for reinforcement. An example of positive contact is: *"Good morning, Jimmy. It's nice to see you!"* An example of positive reinforcement is: *"Jimmy, I saw you helping Susan pick up all the things she spilled out of her backpack. That was very thoughtful. I'm going to give you a positive referral. I want you to know how much I appreciate what you did and how proud I am of you. You should be proud of yourself too! You showed a lot of character."* Notice that the staff member in this last example was very specific about the behavior being rewarded. Also note that the reward was paired with positive adult attention as well as a prompt for the student to acknowledge his own behavior.

Certain practices increase the effectiveness of positive reinforcement. First, reinforcement should be delivered immediately, as close to the target behavior as possible. Any delay in the delivery of a reward lessens the likelihood that the student will associate the reward with the behavior targeted for reinforcement. Time lag between behavior and consequence, whether positive or negative, increases the chance that the consequence may be

paired with an unrelated behavior and decreases or eliminates the effectiveness of the consequence.

Second, positive reinforcement strategies need to be consistent, both with behavior and across staff. Correcting a behavior should also be as consistent as possible. If a student is reinforced for a certain behavior on one occasion, but not on the next, the student may be confused about exactly why he/she is being reinforced. Staff should be especially careful not to reinforce a behavior one time and inadvertently punish it the next time.

Third, positive reinforcement should follow the four-to-one ratio rule. High rates of positive reinforcement have been shown to be highly effective in increasing the likelihood that students will engage in the target behavior.

Basic Instructional Responses for Teaching Behavior

The use of instructional corrective strategies (or responses) for inappropriate or low-level problem behaviors is an effective and efficient first-step response. Instructional responses should be: (a) immediate, (b) contingent on behavior, (c) nonpersonal, nonargumentative, and noncritical, (d) specific to behavior, (e) systematic (correction, model, lead, test, and retest), and (f) consistent (with behavior and across staff).

There are several key features of an effective instructional strategy for teaching expected behavior. First, define what you are teaching. Tell the students exactly what behavior is expected of them. Next, model it. Show the students what it is, what it looks like, and how it's done. Then, lead the students through the behavior sequence. After that, it is critical to have the students *practice* the behavior, making sure that they *correctly* practice the skill(s). It is key to reward or otherwise acknowledge the students for successful practice. If the students still do not "get it" or engage in incorrect practice, it will be necessary to reteach the skill. Finally, it is very important to test the students' mastery of the skill. You can do this by either asking the students to show "the right way" or watching for students using taught skills in natural settings and routines.

After instructional correction for inappropriate behavior, it is important to acknowledge the student's use of the *appropriate* behavior when you see it occurring. Supervisors should watch for students doing what is expected. Actively look for students doing the right things and then reinforce them. Look for progress and attempts by students who are at risk or high risk. Some students need more than one instructional correction and practice sequence before they begin to master the skill. For any student, correct errors immediately by reteaching appropriate behaviors with a consistent delivery of consequences.

In addition, it is highly recommended that supervisors communicate with other staff. Inform other staff concerning both positive and negative behaviors, behavior patterns, intervention problems and successes, etc. A staff that communicates is more consistent and effective in supporting appropriate student behavior and reducing inappropriate behavior.

Immediate and Contingent Delivery of Aversive Consequences (Punishers)

Before correcting inappropriate behavior, be sure you have the facts straight. The following steps are a general guide to delivering effective and efficient consequences:

1. To the greatest extent possible, take the student(s) aside—never reprimand or potentially embarrass students in front of others if you can avoid it.

2. Review what you saw with the student(s) in a calm, businesslike, impersonal manner. Don't argue, and don't be drawn into an argument. Define the problem behavior and establish a clear focus on the appropriate behavior.

3. Ask the student(s) to acknowledge the inappropriate behavior. Ask them to state the appropriate, expected behavior for the situation. If they can't or won't, state the appropriate, expected behavior and ask them to repeat it to you.

4. Give the student(s) choices on how to correct the problem behavior and accept the consequences of inappropriate behavior.

5. Tell the student(s) what the school-prescribed conse-quences for the particular behavior are (use the least aversive consequence indicated for the behavior). Follow school guidelines concerning repeated or chronic violations.

6. Apply the consequence immediately or as soon as practicable.

The Two-Minute Rule for Dealing With Problem Behavior Common areas typically have a high level of student engagement consisting mostly of lightly structured or unstructured student-directed activities, lots of students at any given time, and a high student-to-staff ratio. We call this the "Bees in a Jar" scenario. Students have been engaged in various, relatively highly structured/high-demand, academic and curricular activities preceding recess, lunch, or free time. They are typically restless and ready for social and recreational activities. They are like bees in a jar, cooped up in classrooms until we "open the lid" and tell them to go outside and have fun, but "don't do this and don't do that," etc.

Staff supervising these areas need to be able to quickly, efficiently, and effectively convert problem behavior. Supervisors may have anywhere from 50–100 students to each adult present during a 15- or 20-minute recess. These numbers imply that supervisors can ill afford to spend 5, 10, or even 15 minutes trying to correct a problem. When a supervisor is engaged with a student or group of students, that supervisor is effectively "out of the picture" in terms of supervising and supporting the remaining students, areas, and activities. The need for the supervisor to be able to correct a problem and move on has led to the development of the Two-Minute Rule. Simply put, if a supervisor can't successfully correct a problem behavior within one or two minutes, that problem should be referred to an alternate setting/staff member for processing. If a student is compliant when confronted with a correction or consequence, the process should take no more than a couple of minutes to complete.

If a student presents defiant, disrespectful, or noncompliant behavior in response to a correction or consequence, then the chances of that particular supervisor being able to successfully get the student back on track in a reasonable time without using threats or intimidation (never recommended) are probably slim to none.

By following these simple steps and prearranging for alternate setting support, common-area supervisors can quickly correct problem behavior or make a determination that the problem needs to be referred to an alternate, more supportive setting.

PROBLEM OCCURS
Supervisor defines problem and gives the student a direction, a correction, and/or a consequence.

Student is compliant	*Student is noncompliant*
Supervisor acknowledges cooperation (thanks, praise, or reward)	Supervisor redirects and gives student choices for compliance (e.g., restate the expected behavior and do it the "right way")

Team-Directed, Data-Based Decision Making and Intervention Implementation

The final feature of an effective systematic supervision program is the team-based element. Team-based interventions are considered more stable over time, and team-driven activities are more sustainable and consistent over time. The team serves three important functions:

1. It serves as the basis for behavioral data collection and analysis.

2. It decides on, develops, and implements intervention plans and activities based on specific behavioral data.

3. It disseminates information about behavior and interventions to the rest of the school community.

Like the schoolwide behavior support team, there are five critical features of an effective supervisor team:

1. Administrative buy-in and support.

2. Regular weekly meetings.

3. Intervention and behavior data collection and analysis.

4. Interstaff participation and communication.

5. Part of a schoolwide behavior support program.

The first and most important readiness feature of an effective and sustainable systematic supervision program is administrator buy-in and support. Without the support, commitment, and participation of the school administration, the effectiveness, viability, and sustainability of a supervisor team is seriously compromised and likely to fail. Likewise, the establishment and maintenance of regular weekly (or in some cases, biweekly) meetings is essential to the functions of the supervisor team, particularly in terms of data collection, data analysis, and intervention planning. Intervention planning, development, and implementation, and behavior data collection and analysis are the most important functions of the supervisor team. Without effectively performing these activities, subsequent behavior support measures will be, at best, happenstance and, at worst, detrimental.

Another function of the supervisor team is participation and communication between staff members. Effective behavior support activities are based on schoolwide programs. This implies that all staff participate and effectively communicate with all other members of the school community. Communication between, and participation of, all school staff will help ensure that critical element of consistency across settings and staff that is so integral to successful behavior support programs. Finally, the supervisor team and its activities should be viewed as an important part of a schoolwide behavior support effort.

Review of Establishing Rules for Common Areas

After this detailed look the active supervision program features, it may be useful to revisit the elementary, middle school, and high school **Rules and Behavioral Expectations for Common Areas** matrices from Chapter 5. Take a minute or two to look over the example rule grids from the various grade levels. Think about how you might facilitate the development of school rules and behavior expectations that are unique to common areas such as playgrounds, hallways, cafeterias, etc.

Here are some reminders:

- Rules should be stated in behavioral terms, that is, as what the behavior looks like. For example, "Students will walk in the hallway," not, "Students will behave in the hallway" or "No running."

- Rules should be posted in all school environments (hallways, classrooms, the school handbook, agenda planners, etc).

- Rules should be taught directly to students with formal and specific lessons.

- Rules should be retaught and reviewed at least 10–20 times per year.

Activity: Develop Supervision-Friendly Common-Area Rules

1. Take out a copy of the **Defining Schoolwide Expectations Worksheet** (from Chapter 5) and work with your supervisor team (or other pertinent group).

2. Use the umbrella rules (Be Safe, Be Responsible, and Be Respectful).

3. Make a list of the specific common areas to be addressed (e.g., playground, hallways, cafeteria, etc.).

4. Pick one common area setting for which your team will define the expectations and complete the behavior expectation matrix for that setting.

Review of Teaching School Rules and Behavior Expectations

School rules and expectations are typically taught in context (e.g., hallway, cafeteria, bus, classroom, playground, etc.) at least once toward the beginning of the school year and 10 to 20 times a year in the classroom. It should be noted, however, that common-area behavior may need additional support in terms of teaching and practice in context. That is the main reason to use instructional corrections as the universal consequence for low-level minor misbehavior. In addition, common-area supervisors may find it both necessary and beneficial to use a more formal lesson plan (the **Expected Behavior Lesson Plan** in Chapter 6) when minor problem behavior is being consistently exhibited by most students, misbehavior rates are high, or before certain times of the year when increased minor misbehavior is anticipated in a specific common area.

Staff often focus on punishing disruptive behavior, but students with behavior problems will not make meaningful educational or behavioral progress unless they are taught skills that increase their ability to function in the various school areas.

Review of Reinforcement Systems

A token economy (e.g., Pride Bucks, Gotcha Being Good Tickets, etc.) or perhaps tangibles (candy, sports cards, etc.) coupled with specific adult praise is a simple way of creating a consistent system of positive reinforcement. When used in combination with planned ignoring (see Chapter 13), tokens have been proven effective in reducing acting-out behavior.

The reinforcement system for common areas should be an extension of the schoolwide reinforcement system. All children in the school should have access to positive reinforcement, even those who "challenge" the system.

Behavior is lawful; it happens for a reason. Behavior is functional; it serves a purpose. A person is likely to use behaviors that provide access to rewards that, in turn, increase the likelihood of that behavior recurring. To be useful, behaviors should be effective and efficient. This holds true for inappropriate as well as appropriate behavior. Effective interventions address the functionality of the problem behavior and make it inefficient and less functional than some form of acceptable replacement behavior.

Rewards should be made public (except for those students whom experience has shown are embarrassed or somehow punished by public acknowledgement). Public display and delivery of rewards has a powerful modeling effect, a kind of collateral reinforcement. When students see their peers get rewarded for good behavior, they are often motivated to display the same behaviors.

Implementing a Reward System on the Playground and/or Common Areas

There are six issues to consider when implementing a schoolwide reward system on the playground or in other common areas. By addressing these issues and planning for them, the staff can help assure a successful application of the schoolwide reward and reinforcement system. The six issues are:

1. Attend to behavior you want.

2. Pick your battles.

3. Practice consistency.

4. Use rewards that students want.

5. Increase reinforcement before difficult times.

6. Initiate reteaching of expected behaviors if inappropriate behavior is increasing.

Planning should include attention to how rewards will be distributed and how or where backup rewards will be obtained. Proactive planning should also consider the possible barriers or problems in implementing the system in these common areas. In addition, it is always good to have established backup rewards lined up. Like anyone, students may get tired of a single type of reward, especially middle and high school students.

Assessing Common-Area Needs

Just like the schoolwide portion of the *Best Behavior* Self-Assessment Survey conducted in Chapter 4, it is necessary to focus special attention on common areas. The following **Checklist for Common-Area Supervision** is designed to support team planning and goal setting around common-area supervision plans. Complete the assessment with your colleagues and then set improvement goals and systematic supervision plans. We recommend using the checklist to target specific objectives for improving common-area supervision. For example, if you rate item 4 (rocks and sticks on the playground) as extensive, then a plan to remove those hazards should be carried out.

Checklist for Common-Area Supervision

School _____ Date _____

Indicate to what extent you think the items or features listed are present in your school common areas using the following 1–4 scale, where:

1 = Not at all . . . 4 = Extensive

Circle your response keeping in mind that the Environmental Items and Features address positive attributes and the Behavioral Concerns address negative issues.

Environmental Items and Features

1. Common areas are easily observable (unobstructed views) from any given position in the area. 1 2 3 4

2. It is easy for supervisors to make close physical contact with students in all common areas. 1 2 3 4

3. Playground or recess equipment is safe. 1 2 3 4

4. Rocks, sticks, or other potentially dangerous or hazardous objects or materials are present on the playground, or other common areas. 1 2 3 4

5. Access to and from the playground, recess, or free-time areas is easily supervised. 1 2 3 4

6. Transition to and from the common area is safe and efficient (quick, orderly, supervised, established routes and behaviors, etc.). 1 2 3 4

7. Procedures and behavioral expectations for all students entering and exiting common areas have been developed, taught to all, and practiced. 1 2 3 4

8. Formal emergency or crisis procedures for students and staff on playgrounds or in other common areas have been developed and are practiced at least twice a year. 1 2 3 4

9. There is adequate staff in common areas (playgrounds, during recess and free time, etc.) to effectively supervise the number of students present. 1 2 3 4

10. Supervisors have a common attention signal or other cue that signals students when it is time to transition, stop activities, etc. 1 2 3 4

11. Common-area supervision staff have been trained in active supervision techniques and methods this year. 1 2 3 4

12. A system of positive reinforcement is in place in all common-area settings. 1 2 3 4

89

1 = Not at all . . . 4 = Extensive

13. Common-area supervision staff has weekly or biweekly team meetings (includes a school administrator). 1 2 3 4

14. A system for addressing minor problem behavior in common areas (during recess, on the playground, etc.) is in place and practiced by all common-area supervision staff. 1 2 3 4

15. A system for addressing serious or major problem behavior in recess, playground, or common areas is in place and practiced by all common-area supervision staff. 1 2 3 4

16. Off-limits areas are clearly identified, taught to students and staff, and known by all. 1 2 3 4

17. Students are permitted access to unsupervised areas during recess or free time. 1 2 3 4

Behavioral Concerns

18. Student-to-student arguing is a problem. 1 2 3 4

19. Students engage in "hands on others" (grabbing, "rodeo hugs," etc.). 1 2 3 4

20. Students engage in play fighting. 1 2 3 4

21. Students engage in rough play (pushing, shoving, tackling, etc.). 1 2 3 4

22. Students use disrespectful language with and against their peers. 1 2 3 4

23. Students violate or ignore school playground, recess, free-time, or other common-area behavioral expectations or rules. 1 2 3 4

24. Students ignore playground, recess, free-time, or other common-area game rules. 1 2 3 4

25. Students tease other students. 1 2 3 4

26. Students engage in name calling or other personally offensive language with other students. 1 2 3 4

27. Students limit-test with supervisors. 1 2 3 4

28. Students are overtly disrespectful and defiant with supervisors. 1 2 3 4

29. Students verbally or physically threaten other students. 1 2 3 4

1 = Not at all . . . 4 = Extensive

30. Students engage in illegal activities (i.e., alcohol, tobacco, drugs, weapon carrying, etc.). 1 2 3 4

31. Students fight physically with each other. 1 2 3 4

32. Students bully and harass each other. 1 2 3 4

33. Students verbally or physically threaten supervisors. 1 2 3 4

34. Supervisors are afraid of, or intimidated by, some students. 1 2 3 4

35. Certain activities or games are more challenging in terms of student behavior than others. 1 2 3 4

Structured or Semistructured Activities and/or Games

List the structured or semistructured activities and/or games present in your school, (e.g., tetherball, wall ball, soccer, basketball, etc.) and rate the extent to which they are a setting for problem behavior:

1. _____

   _____ 1 2 3 4

2. _____

   _____ 1 2 3 4

3. _____

   _____ 1 2 3 4

4. _____

   _____ 1 2 3 4

5. _____

   _____ 1 2 3 4

6. _____

   _____ 1 2 3 4

7. _____

   _____ 1 2 3 4

1 = Not at all . . . 4 = Extensive

8. _____

_____   1 2 3 4

9. _____

_____   1 2 3 4

10. _____

_____   1 2 3 4

11. _____

_____   1 2 3 4

12. _____

_____   1 2 3 4

13. _____

_____   1 2 3 4

14. _____

_____   1 2 3 4

15. _____

_____   1 2 3 4

16. _____

_____   1 2 3 4

17. _____

_____   1 2 3 4

18. _____

_____   1 2 3 4

19. _____

_____   1 2 3 4

20. _____

_____   1 2 3 4

chapter 9

Using Discipline Referrals to Diagnose Schoolwide and Individual Student Needs

Chapter Objectives:

○ Describe features of an effective discipline referral system

○ Review and revise your system for office discipline referrals

○ Discuss increasing consistency of discipline referral procedures

○ Identify program needs based on referral data patterns

Schools that are safe, effective, and violence free are not accidents. They are environments where considerable effort has been made to build and maintain supportive school cultures. Part of the effort consists of evaluating and monitoring the types of behaviors students are exhibiting.

How Schools Use Discipline Referrals

Office discipline referrals are used by schools as one method for managing and monitoring disruptive behavior. Referrals are more than an index of student behavior. They are an index of the consistency and quality of the school discipline system. The major advantage of discipline referrals is that they are already collected in most schools and provide a source of information to document whether interventions result in positive change (Skiba et al., 1997; Tobin, Sugai, & Colvin, 2000; Walker, Stieber, Ramsey, & O'Neill, 1993; Wright & Dusek, 1998).

We must be cautious when using discipline referrals as a source of information about behaviors. Each school defines and applies referral procedures differently. Just because a school has a high rate of referrals does not necessarily mean that the students are less well behaved than the students at another school with fewer referrals. The same student may evoke different responses from teachers in different schools, and different relation-ships between teachers and administrators will affect the use of discipline referrals across schools. Despite these cautions, office referral data is useful in identifying discipline patterns of students (Wright & Dusek, 1998), identifying the effects of schoolwide and classroom interventions (Metzler et al., 2001; Taylor-Greene et al., 1997) and staff training needs (Tobin et al., 2000).

Many of us are accustomed to looking at data on individual student performance. It also is useful to look at data on the performance of the whole school or a particular classroom regarding discipline referrals. We can use discipline referrals to identify problem areas in the school, determine if interventions are working, and identify problem students.

Many schools use referral data for decision making. They use regular cycles of data collection and reporting, such as daily recording of each referral, monthly feedback to staff, and annual updating of the system and revising as needed. If the data are consistent and useful, people will use them! We must also ensure that the process is efficient (low effort, time, and cost). Please take a moment with the following reflection to think about your school's use of discipline referral.

Reflection

My School's Discipline Referral Data

1. How is discipline referral data used in my school?

2. What are some concerns about using discipline referrals to make school discipline decisions?

3. What are some practices that make use of discipline referrals effective?

4. How often do I get information about discipline referral patterns from my administrator?

5. What needs to be improved in our office discipline referral system?

The process for using referral data is not complex, but it is important that all staff in the building agree to use the process in the same way. Please refer to the sample referral forms elsewhere in this chapter and examine their features. The **Behavior Referral Form**, **Referral Notice**, **Student Citation Form**, and **Notice to Parents of Disciplinary Action Form** are examples of good referral forms.

The following box lists the basic elements of the referral form.

Referral Form Elements

- Date and time

- Student name

- Student grade

- Cause of the referral (the behavior)

- Location of the referral

- Referring staff member

- Response or consequence for the student

What to Look at: The Key Indicators

We look at the key indicators to examine discipline referral patterns. Each of the summary statistics is easy to derive and tells a lot about what is happening in the school. The following chart provides a summary of each indicator.

Office Discipline Referrals: Key Indicators

- Total number of office discipline referrals

- Referrals per enrolled student

- Average referrals per school day per month

- Location of referrals (e.g., common areas of classrooms)

- Percentage of students with 0–1 referrals

- Percentage of students with 2–6 referrals

- Percentage of students with 7 or more referrals

We will now begin to look at how these data can really guide our discipline program decision making by finding successes and trouble spots. We have found that the following rules are useful:

- *Schoolwide improvement* is needed when total referrals per year per student is high.

- *Common-area improvement* is needed when there is a specific area of school with more referrals.

- *Classroom management improvement* is needed when there are:

  — More referrals coming from all classrooms.

  — Specific classrooms with more referrals.

- Individual student improvement is needed when:

  — The proportion of students with two to six referrals is high.

  — There are students who have received more than six referrals.

  — There are many suspensions and expulsions.

Activity

Analyzing Office Discipline Referrals (Which System Needs Improvement?)

Now that you have reviewed the decision rules, it is time to practice. This worksheet provides a format for applying the decision rules. Please review the table below and indicate on the worksheet which school needs improvement in each area and why.

Activity Chart

School	Grades	# of Referrals	Referrals per Student	Referrals per Day per Month	% From Classroom	% From Common Area	% With 2–6 Referrals	% With 7 or More Referrals
A	K–5	250	.90	1.5	25	20	32	4
B	K–6	331	.50	1.9	28	50	12	1.5
C	6–8	3520	3.0	20.6	30	25	35	1
D	9–12	1300	.90	7.6	50	15	20	8

Activity Worksheet

1. Schoolwide system improvement is indicated when the average number of referrals per day is high (>2 elementary, >6 middle, >8 high school). **Which school(s) in the chart has this need and why?**

   _____

   _____

   _____

2. Common area improvement is indicated when 30% or more of all referrals come from a specific setting. **Which school(s) in the chart has this need and why?**

   _____

   _____

   _____

3. Classroom management improvement is indicated when 40% or more referrals come from all classrooms or there are specific classrooms with more referrals. **Which school(s) in the chart has this need and why?**

   _____

   _____

   _____

4. Individual student improvement is indicated when: (a) the proportion of students with 2 to 6 referrals is high, (b) there are students who have received >6 referrals, and (c) there is a high frequency of suspensions and expulsions. **Which school(s) in the chart has this need and why?**

   _____

   _____

   _____

Best Behavior • **chapter nine**

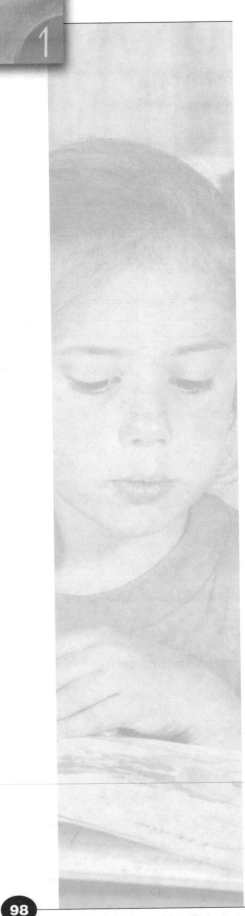

Activity Answer Key

1. C. This school needs schoolwide improvement because it has a high number of overall referrals and referrals per day.

2. B. This school needs common-area improvement because 50% of all referrals originate from there.

3. D. This school needs classroom management improvement because 50% of all referrals originate from classrooms.

4. C and/or D. School C has a high proportion of students with 2–6 referrals and School D has a high proportion of students with 7 or more.

Behavior Referral Form

Student Name: _____

Teacher: _____ Referring Staff: _____

Grade: K 1 2 3 4 5 6   Date: _____   Time: _____

Location	Problem Behavior	Possible Motivation	Adminstrative Action
__ Arrival/dismissal area	__ Damage to property	__ Peer attention	*For Office Use Only:*
__ Bus loading area	__ Defiance/disrespect	__ Adult attention	__ Review of school rules
__ Cafeteria/quad	__ Disruption	__ Obtain items/activities	__ Loss of privilege
__ Classroom	__ Inappropriate language	__ Avoid peer(s)	__ Recess/lunch detention
__ Library/pod area	__ Physical aggression	__ Avoid adult(s)	from _____
__ Office	__ Tease/threaten/harass	__ Avoid task/activity	to _____
__ On bus	__ Other (specify)	__ Don't know	__ Time out in office
__ Passing areas		__ Other (specify)	from _____
__ Playground			to _____
__ Restrooms			__ Suspension for ____ day(s)
__ Special event/assembly			__ Other (specify)
__ Other (specify)			_____
			__ Parent Contact Y N

Others involved in incident:

___ None   ___ Peer(s)   ___ Staff   ___ Teacher   ___ Substitute   ___ Other   ___ Unknown

If peers were involved, list them: _____

_____

Classroom management steps taken today to address behavior:

___ None   ___ Warned; rules reviewed   ___ Loss of recess/privilege   ___ Time out

___ Phone call   ___ Other (specify) _____

Last documented contact with parent/guardian:

___ Conference at school   ___ Phone call   Date of contact: _____

Other comments:

_____

_____

_____

_____

_____

Administrator Signature   Date

_____

Parent/Guardian Signature   Date

Referral Notice

Period: AM 1 2 3 4 5 6 7 8 PM

Name _____ Time _____

Location: Class   Grounds   Commons Hall/Breezeway   Cafeteria   Restroom   Gym   Library
Bus Area   Parking Lot   Bus   Special Event   Other (specify) _____

Staff _____ Grade _____ Time _____

○ Counseling   ○ Behavior   ○ Attendance   ○ Severe

Action Taken by Office:

Previous Teacher or Team Action:

Description of Problem:

Motivation:
○ Obtain peer attention
○ Obtain adult attention
○ Obtain items/activities
○ Avoid tasks/activities
○ Avoid peer(s)
○ Avoid adult(s)
○ Don't know
○ Other (specify)

_____
_____
_____
_____
_____

Administrative Decision:
○ Passroom   ○ Detention
○ Parent Contact   ○ Loss of Privilege
○ Ind. Instruction ○ In-School Susp.
○ Conference   ○ Saturday School
○ Out-of-School Susp.

Others Involved: ○ Staff ○ Peers ○ None ○ Unknown

○ Parent contact by phone

Signature _____   Date/Time _____

White: Parent / Yellow: Office / Pink: Teacher / Goldenrod: Teacher

Student Citation Form

Student: _____

Grade: ___ Time: _____ Date: _____

Referring Person: _____

Teacher: _____

This student has had problems:

__ Being SAFE

__ Being KIND

__ Being PRODUCTIVE

Specific problems include:

__ Aggressive Play

__ Vandalism

__ Unsafe Play

__ Defiance/Disruption

__ Bullying

__ Harassment

__ Inappropriate Language

__ Fighting

__ Cruel Teasing

__ Obscenity

Other: _____

_____

_____

_____

_____

_____

_____

_____

_____

Parent Signature

Student Citation Form

Student: _____

Grade: ___ Time: _____ Date: _____

Referring Person: _____

Teacher: _____

This student has had problems:

__ Being SAFE

__ Being KIND

__ Being PRODUCTIVE

Specific problems include:

__ Aggressive Play

__ Vandalism

__ Unsafe Play

__ Defiance/Disruption

__ Bullying

__ Harassment

__ Inappropriate Language

__ Fighting

__ Cruel Teasing

__ Obscenity

Other: _____

_____

_____

_____

_____

_____

_____

_____

_____

Parent Signature

101

Notice to Parents of Disciplinary Action Form

Student Name: _____ Grade: _____

Referring Staff: _____ Date: _____ Time: _____ Day: M T W T F

Location

__ Classroom	__ Commons: Cafe. __ Rec. __	__ On Bus/Van
__ School Store	__ Computer Center	__ Bike Rack
__ Hallway	__ Library	__ Assembly/Activity
__ Front desk	__ Parking Lot/Driveway	__ Service Learning

Problem Behaviors

__ Abusive/Inappropriate Language/Gesture	__ Harassment/Tease/Taunt/ Bullying/Name Calling	__ Theft/Stealing
__ Fighting or Physical Aggression	__ Disruption _____	__ Lying/Cheating
__ Defiance _____	__ Tardy	__ Vandalism
__ Disrespect _____	__ Skipping Class/Out of Area	__ Property Damage
		__ False Alarm

Possible Motivation

__ Obtain Peer Attention	__ Avoid Peers
__ Obtain Adult Attention	__ Avoid Adults
__ Obtain Items/Activities	__ Don't Know

Others Involved

__ None	__ Substitute
__ Peers	__ Unknown
__ Staff	__ Other _____
__ Teacher _____	

Administrative Decision

__ Time in Office	__ Recess Detention/Structure or Alternative Recess	__ Out-of-School Suspension
__ Loss of Privilege	__ Individualized Instruction	__ Other _____
__ Conference With Student	__ In-School Suspension	__ Referral to SST
__ Parent Contact		__ Written Acknowledgment/ Apology

Comments: _____

Dates Parent Contacted _____ School Official Signature _____

Parent Follow-up

Thank you for your support in encouraging positive behavior at school! Please talk to your child about his or her behavior in this incident. If you have any questions, please contact us at _____.

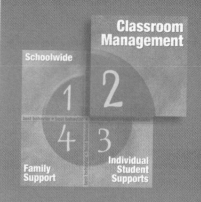

Classroom Management

Schoolwide
best behavior • best behavior
1
2
4
3
Family Support
Individual Student Supports

Classroom Management

chapter ten

Classroom Organization: The Foundation of Classroom Management

Chapter Objectives:

○ Describe the organization of an effective classroom

○ Evaluate your classroom environment

○ Set goals for improving your classroom environment

The focus up to this point has been on universal, schoolwide strategies such as social skills training, positive feedback systems, active supervision, and behavior monitoring through office discipline referral patterns. Without the universal system in place, classroom management is less effective. The universal discipline system that the school develops is the basis for your classroom management, providing the guidelines and expectations for all students anywhere in the school, including your classroom. It creates consistent procedures and language for all staff when reinforcing or correcting students.

Most teachers, however, want specific expectations and routines in their classroom. While the teacher has the most control over her classroom and her behavior within it, classroom management should be consistent with the schoolwide system. The expectations you develop, teach, and recognize should be taught in the same manner as the schoolwide expectations. Any reward and recognition system you create should work on the same principles as the schoolwide system.

Effective Classroom Organization

An effective classroom environment begins with classroom organization. Teachers need strategies for teaching appropriate behavior and managing problem behaviors in the classroom. This work should begin before the start of the school year. Teachers must establish a structured classroom environment that encourages appropriate behavior and fosters learning. Effective classroom managers know what they want to see in their classroom throughout the day (entering, leaving, transitions, and independent work), and what they want to hear from their students (noise level, being respectful, asking for help). Effective teachers do not assume that students instinctively know what is expected. They explicitly teach and provide positive and constructive feedback until the behavior becomes an automatic part of the daily classroom routine. The following reflection presents a few questions you should think about regarding classroom management.

Reflection

Classroom Management

1. List five or more important features of the class-room environment to which a teacher must pay attention before the school year starts.

2. What are some good classroom rules (positively stated, easy to remember) that link with your school rules?

3. List two or more classroom-management activities to which teachers must attend on the first day of school.

4. What would you do if two or three students in a class of 30 constantly disrupted the class?

5. Name two strategies you would use to keep all students on task during independent work.

Before the school year begins, you need to plan the physical arrangement of the classroom. You must be able to:

- Monitor students at all times (no groups or students behind bookcases or dividers).

- Gain physical access to all students (sufficient space between desks).

- Place high-need and low-performing students where you have easy access for reinforcement and feedback.

- Decide seat assignments or provide choice seating.

- Decide where you want the teacher desk and who has access to it.

After deciding where you want your desk, your students' desks, other working areas, and material and equipment storage, it will be easier for you to deal with the many demands and challenges you will be facing after the students arrive. Plan for uncluttered bulletin board areas. Use semipermanent thematic displays (e.g., Animals, Insects, Plants, Countries, Cultures, Transportation) and permanent areas to display student work, schedules, and writing guidelines (e.g., paper headings) to save time. When you have a clear picture of the physical aspects of your classroom, think a few moments about what you would like your ideal classroom to look like in action. Then, take a look at the following example.

Example

Imagine students arriving in the morning, quietly sitting down, starting a warm-up activity, and working respectfully until all students have arrived and you give a transition signal. Your students change groups efficiently and respectfully. When they arrive at their next subject area, they are equipped with appropriate books, paper, and pencils and are ready to follow directions. While you instruct, everyone can see you and everyone listens respectfully. During independent work time, your students know how to work quietly, access help, and obtain materials. You circulate among the students and provide them with positive feedback and corrective feedback. At lunchtime, your students get ready efficiently, orderly, and respectfully.

The images in the example form the basis for your classroom expectations. You are going to define and teach your students how to live up to your expectations. We will examine developing and teaching classroom expectations in Chapter 11. First we recommend that you think about and complete the following **Classroom Organization Checklist**. The checklist asks questions, which you can answer in the space provided. For those items you feel are complete or in place, just check in the box to the right. When you are finished, decide which areas need improvement.

Classroom Organization Checklist

1. Teacher's desk

- Where is it? _____
  _____ ○

- How are students allowed to use your desk? _____
  _____ ○

- How do you monitor the entire class when you are at your desk? _____
  _____ ○

- What is the procedure for items that need your attention immediately? _____
  _____ ○

- Can students come up to you when you are at your desk? _____
  _____ ○

- If you have a phone at your desk, what are the rules regarding use? _____
  _____ ○

- What other expectations do you have regarding your desk? _____
  _____ ○

2. Material storage

- Where are frequently used supplies stored? _____
  _____ ○

- Where are textbooks stored? Are the ones you use daily easily accessible? _____
  _____ ○

- Do you experience problems associated with supplies? _____
  _____ ○

- What are some solutions to these problems? _____
  _____ ○

- Where do you store seasonal or infrequently used materials? _____
  _____ ○

3. Start of class procedures

- What are students expected to do when they enter the room (e.g., warm-up activity, go to desk
  and read quietly, etc.)? _____
  _____ ○

4. General classroom procedures

Complete?

- What can students do if they finish independent work early? _____

  _____ ○

- When can students sharpen pencils? _____

  _____ ○

- What do students do when their pencil breaks or another writing tool is needed? _____

  _____ ○

- What do students do when they need supplies while working on independent work? _____

  _____ ○

- What are bathroom procedures? Are there designated times? Can students obtain a pass?

  _____ ○

- What procedures need to be followed to go to the office, nurse, counselor, etc.? _____

  _____ ○

6. Independent work procedures

- What are students expected to do during independent seatwork? _____

  _____ ○

- Can students leave their seats? _____

  _____ ○

- Can students talk to each other? _____

  _____ ○

- Can students interact with the teacher? _____

  _____ ○

- How do students ask for assistance? _____

  _____ ○

- What do students do when the assignment is finished? _____

  _____ ○

7. Transitions

- How do students move from one activity to another? _____

  _____ ○

- How do students move from one classroom to another? _____

  _____ ○

8. Dismissal procedures

Complete?

- How are students dismissed to go to break, lunch, or other activities? _____
  _____ ○

- What procedures are in place for end-of-school dismissal? _____
  _____ ○

9. Homework policy

- Do you have a homework policy? _____ ○

- Where do students write down the assignment? _____ ○

- Do students have homework assignment envelopes, agenda planners, or notebooks?
  _____ ○

- Where do students turn in completed homework assignments? _____
  _____ ○

- What is your record-keeping system for assignments? _____
  _____ ○

- What happens when students don't turn in completed work? _____
  _____ ○

- What is your reinforcement system for completed homework (e.g., points, grades, free homework pass)? _____
  _____ ○

- What are procedures for chronic homework problems? _____
  _____ ○

10. Common problem procedures

- What happens when a student talks out in class? _____
  _____ ○

- What happens when a student gets out of seat without permission? _____
  _____ ○

11. Computer procedures

- When and how long can students use the computer? _____
  _____ ○

- What are your expectations about water, food, gum, etc.? _____
  _____ ○

111

12. Quiet time areas

- What is your procedure for a student who works better in a quiet, less distracting area? Is there a quiet Is there reading corner (e.g., bean bag, rocking chair)? _____ _____ ○

- What is your procedure for a student who has lost the privilege to be part of the class for a short period of time? Can students go to another teacher's classroom when they have lost the privilege to be in your room?_____ _____ ○

- What is your procedure for students who have to be in in-school suspension? _____ _____ ○

- How and when will you teach your students about the quiet-time procedures?_____ _____ ○

13. Parent contact policies

- What is your plan for contacting parents?_____ _____ ○

- What are your procedures to let parents know when things are going well? _____ _____ ○

- What do you do when things are not going well? _____ _____ ○

Before selecting areas in your classroom that need fine tuning, please examine the **Sample Classroom Organization Form** in Figure 16. Then, complete the blank **Classroom Organization Form**.

Figure 16

Sample Classroom Organization Form

Procedures:	Particulars:
Pick one area that needs improvement in your classroom	It bothers me when students yell when they need my attention or when they come up to me and interrupt while I am helping other students.
Write what you want to see instead	I would like my students to notice when I am available for attention and raise their hands quietly.
Write how you will teach your students the new expectation	
Use examples	Say: "When you need attention, look and see if I am talking to another student. When I am finished talking, raise your hand quietly and wait for me to call on you. Like this." Demonstrate.
Nonexamples	Wave your hand and yell: "Teacher, teacher!" Say: "Is that the right way to get my attention?" or "Walk up to me and say: 'I don't know how to do this.' That is not the right way. Let me show you the right way one more time."

Classroom Organization Form

Procedures:	Particulars:
Pick one area that needs improvement in your classroom	
Write what you want to see instead	
Write how you will teach your students the new expectation	
Use examples	
Nonexamples	

chapter 11

Designing and Teaching Classroom Behavioral Expectations

Chapter Objectives:

❍ Describe how classroom rules contribute to effective classroom management

❍ Develop a few positive classroom rules

If the teacher does not know exactly what to expect in the classroom and how to communicate it, neither will the students. Students should know when they can talk quietly and when they need to be silent. They must understand how to be respectful to others. If the teacher expects no talking while a student raises his hand, anything less is not acceptable. Otherwise, students will learn that expectations are flexible and can be broken. The emphasis when developing effective classroom expectations is on clarity, consistency, and precision.

Building Blocks for Classroom Discipline

As with schoolwide expectations, classroom expectations should be short and simple so

students can remember them. Expectations are the building blocks for your classroom discipline plan so be sure to devote as much time and energy as possible to forming an effective list. If you have a clear idea of what the boundaries are in your classroom, and you consistently enforce those boundaries, many problem behaviors will disappear or be prevented.

Classroom expectations are used in several ways. First, you describe and teach the expectations the first few days of school. You need to provide your students with a rationale for each rule and discuss how following the rule can help with being safe, responsible, and/or respectful. Second, when you provide specific feedback on following the expectations, students learn what it means to be safe, responsible, and/or respectful. Examples might be: *"Nico, I noticed that you brought your notebook and pencil to group. That's responsible." "You were sitting quietly while I was talking. That's respectful." "You remembered to walk down the hallway. That's being safe."*

It is helpful if the umbrella expectations (e.g., be safe, be responsible, and be respectful) are defined and made into posters placed at eye level in the classroom. A posted set of expectations provides a message that certain behaviors are very important to you. Students also can put a copy of the expectations in their notebooks or taped onto their desks. One copy may be sent home to be returned with a parent's signature.

Finally, you can remind students of following the expectations and engaging in appropriate behavior throughout the year by providing booster activities such as reteaching a lesson, posting new expectations posters, or changing the incentive for following the expectations. For example, you might initiate "Responsibility Week" and reward students for success with extra lunch time or other incentives you choose or negotiate with the students.

Practice those expectations that are frequently broken by many students in the class. When several students have a difficult time following expectations, a classwide motivational system can be very effective (see Chapter 13). Individual students who are having a hard time following classroom expectations need to be encouraged to keep trying. A teacher could say, for example, *"Sometimes it's really hard to remember all the expectations in school. You are working on it and I am sure you will get it."*

If a student has chronic problems, the teacher should privately ask the student what might be done to change the situation and perhaps agree on a positive plan to help the student be more successful. Extra-challenging behavior problems will require more intense planning and support to achieve success (see Chapter 15 for techniques to "think functionally" about challenging behavior).

Expectations and procedures might vary from teacher to teacher, but effective teachers have very clear expectations. It is very difficult to run an effective classroom if there are no clear expectations about walking around in the room, interrupting the teacher, or working productively. In addition, inefficient procedures and lack of automatic classroom routines can waste enormous amounts of time and take away from valuable instructional time (Carnine, Silbert, & Kameenui, 1997; Hofmeister & Lubke, 1990; Latham, 1992).

Develop Your Classroom Expectations

The expectations you choose should reflect how you want your students to behave at all times. If your schoolwide umbrella expectations are to be safe, be responsible, and be respectful, define what that looks like in your classroom and explicitly teach it. When you define expectations, it is helpful to ask the following two questions:

1. What do you want to see?

2. What do you want to hear?

The following activity provides a way to come up with your expectations. Be careful not to fall into the trap of saying; "*My students would never be able to do what I would like to see or hear,*" or "*My students come from such diverse backgrounds; they could never show the kind of respect I want.*" If your expectations are very clear and taught well, your students will do what you expect of them. It is especially important to have very high expectations for students from inconsistent, unpredictable home environments. They will rise to the occasion. It helps them feel safe and gives them a sense of belonging when they know exactly what to do or how to act. It makes their school lives predictable. Predictability helps them make good choices

because they know exactly what will happen if they do or don't follow directions.

Activity

Visualizing Success

Close your eyes and visualize your perfect classroom on a perfect day. What do you want to see and hear?

Now open your eyes and write the five most important things you saw and heard.

1. _____

2. _____

3. _____

4. _____

5. _____

After generating a list, get ready to develop your expectations. Remember the following points when making expectations:

- State expectations in a positive way—what behaviors do you want to see?

- Make examples clear and concise.

- Display expectations publicly and at students' eye level.

- Establish and teach classroom expectations immediately—on the first day!

- Teach and review expectations often.

The following **Classroom Expectations Matrix** is intended to help you define your expectations. Refer to the **Classroom Organization Form** in Chapter 10 and write out exactly what you want your students to do for each expectation, then decide whether you want the expectation to go under the column Safe, Respectful, or Responsible. Also, examine the **School Rules and Behavioral Expectations** matrices in Chapter 5.

Classroom Expectations Matrix

Expectations for:	Safe	Respectful	Responsible
Teacher's Desk			
Materials			
Enter and Exit			
Free Time			
Asking for Help			
Quiet Time			
Seat Work			
Drinks			
Bathroom			
Additional Categories			

Teach, Review, and Evaluate Expectations

Teaching classroom expectations is similar to teaching school-wide expectations. One difference is that schoolwide expectations are the same for all students in the building, whereas classroom expectations may vary from classroom to classroom. Expectations should be periodically reviewed, especially during more difficult times (e.g., before or after school breaks or holidays). Instead of allowing things to get out of hand, review the expectations and heavily reinforce those students who are following the expectations.

Expectations that aren't working should be discarded or changed. For example, to avoid excessive movement during independent work time, one of your expectations may be that students will get a number when they need assistance. But the result is that students get up many times during a period to pick a number. The system you developed is not working and should be changed.

Finally, after making and while maintaining expectations, remember the following:

- Review expectations regularly and edit them; don't wait for a crisis.

- Monitor and reinforce when a rule is followed.

- Apply expectations consistently to each and every student.

- If a rule doesn't address a problem, discard it.

chapter 12

Preventive Interactions

Chapter Objectives:

○ Discuss methods to secure students' attention

○ Describe use of direct speech (alpha commands) when interacting with students.

○ Present a specific Predictable Response Sequence to students who are noncompliant

When the physical aspects of your classroom have been examined and behavioral expectations are clear, you need to be prepared for the small percentage of students who will still experience difficulties meeting classroom expectations. Let's begin with a reflection on how you would deal with a few common classroom management challenges.

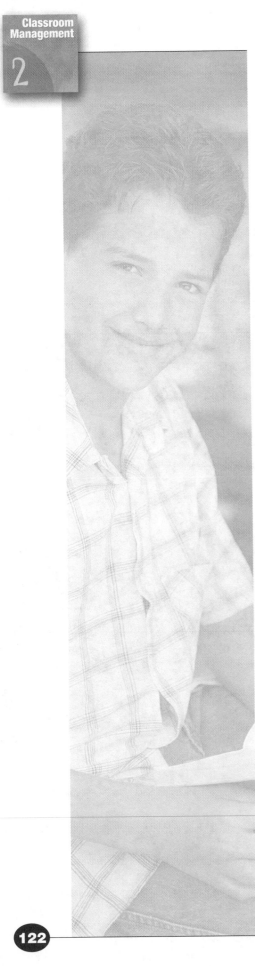

Classroom Management Challenges

Scenario 1: When you need to give directions, many students continue to work on their task and don't hear what you are saying.

How would you deal with this situation?

Scenario 2: One of your students often wanders around the room, bothering other students. You have asked her to sit down and mind her own business. She often ignores your requests, and her peers are annoyed by her behavior.

How would you handle this situation?

Scenario 3: Jose has become very upset and is bothering other students during seat work.

How would you deal with this situation?

Using an Attention Signal (Securing Students' Attention)

For several reasons, we recommend that you use a consistent technique for getting students' attention before giving directions or making announcements: (a) to reduce the need for repetition, (b) to teach students to listen respectfully to others, and (c) to use as a preventive tool for students with challenging behaviors. Through consistent use of an attention signal, students are taught the expectation that when someone talks, respect is shown by stopping activities, being quiet, focusing on the speaker, and listening.

Most teachers have a way to get students' attention, such as a verbal signal, a bell, a xylophone, a clapping rhythm, lights, etc. When students' attention is requested, teachers might encounter a few students who will stop what they are doing for a moment but then will engage in activities other than listening respectfully. If this is the case, the entire class needs to be explicitly taught the idea that: "*When I give an audible signal and say, 'May I have your attention, please?' stop what you are doing, put your eyes on me, and listen until I tell you to go back to work again.*" This skill can be taught in a positive way using a motivational system such as the Concentration/Focus Power Game (see Chapter 13) until students automatically use the skill. Stopping activities and listening quietly when someone talks is a respectful social skill for people of all ages.

When the attention-signal strategy has become an automatic part of classroom procedures, it can be effectively used as a preventive interaction. For example, during independent seatwork several students are bothering others and keeping them off task. If the inappropriate behavior continues, peers may become aggravated, the situation could escalate, and valuable work time will be lost. Instead of drawing attention to the inappropriate behavior, the teacher can give the usual audible signal and say: "*May I have your attention, please?*" After all students are quiet, the teacher can say: "*Thank you for giving me your attention right away. Are there any questions about the assignments? I will come around and see how everyone is doing. I need you to work quietly and respectfully in your groups. You may go back to work now.*" The teacher should not reprimand and single out the small group. The entire class is asked to listen. This strategy provides the problem students a moment to calm down and reassures the rest of the class that the teacher will come and monitor. Here are some steps to help establish and teach an attention-getting system using a variety of modalities:

1. Use an audible signal such as a bell, a musical instrument (e.g., xylophone, harp), or other device to get student attention. Then,

   - Say: "*May I have your attention please?*" or,

   - Say: "*Quiet, please*" while using the audible signal, or,

   - Clap your hands in a pattern and have the children repeat the pattern.

2. Demonstrate clear examples and nonexamples of what students must do when they hear the signal.

- Example: Stop what you are doing and look at the teacher without talking.

- Nonexample: Continue to work or talk.

- Nonexample: Stop for a moment, then continue to work.

- Example: Walk through the room and stop immediately while looking at the teacher.

3. Ask students for feedback after each example scenario.

- Ask: "*Did I do it the right way? Why or why not?*"

4. When practicing or using the skill, immediately recognize students who are doing it correctly. For example:

- "*When I asked for your attention, you followed directions right away. That's showing respect.*"

5. Practice with a stopwatch until all students give attention within 30 seconds. Continue to practice for a few days until the skill is firm.

6. Continue to reinforce students until the behavior is automatic.

If some students are not following directions despite your teaching clear expectations:

1. Minimize attention for the behavior. When it happens the first time, focus on students who are doing it right.

2. If it happens several times, talk to the student alone during a quiet, positive time and say something like: "*It seems to be difficult for you to stop what you are doing and listen to me quietly when I give the attention signal. Is there anything I can do to help you follow directions right away?* (Listen to response). *Today I will watch and see how you do. I will appreciate your help.*" Follow up if the student cooperates.

3. If a student continues to have problems, speak to the student alone away from peers and set up a time to role play one on one when you and the student can be alone. It may be necessary to set up an individual incentive for the student.

Reducing and Preventing Noncompliance
With Direct Speech (Alpha Commands)

Noncompliance is simply defined as not following a direction within a reasonable amount of time. Most arguing, tantrums, fighting, or rule breaking are secondary to avoiding requests or required tasks. Following directions is essential for success in school and society. This basic skill is often overlooked by educators, and can be a key issue for many students with behavior problems. Whether or not a child complies with an adult directive has as much to do with how the command is framed and delivered as it does with the consequences (or lack of them) that follow the delivery (Walker & Walker, 1991).

When students are misbehaving, teachers must give clear and concise directions on what the students need to be doing, not what they should not be doing. Clear and positive directions are called alpha commands. An example of an alpha command might be "*Pick up your chair, sit down, and draw a picture of your favorite animal,*" instead of "*How many times have I told you not to get up out of your seat. Don't you know how to act in this class? I'm getting tired of telling you what to do a hundred times. Now, get to work.*" The latter is an example of a beta command. This beta command does not give the student specific information on what needs to be done. It also conveys signs of frustration from the teacher. Figure 17 outlines the differences between the two command types.

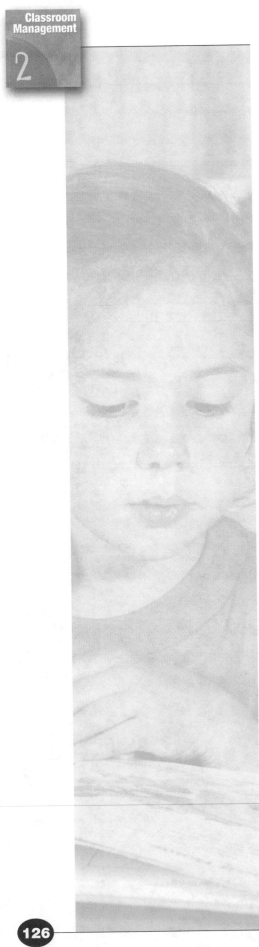

Figure 17

Alpha and Beta Commands

Alpha Commands:

- Minimal number of words

- Clear, concrete, and specific

- Reasonable amount of time for behavior to occur

Beta Commands:

- Wordy

- Vague

- Often convey feelings of frustration or anger

- May contain many sets of directions

Now that you have reviewed the definitions and importance of using clear speech, set a time to complete the following activity to practice using alpha and beta commands.

Activity

Alpha and Beta Role Play

- Invite another person to practice with you. One person (A) role plays being a teacher; the other person (B) role plays being a student.

- Person A uses an alpha command; person B follows the directions.

- Person A uses a beta command for the same situation; person B follows the directions.

- Discuss the difference between the first and the second command.

Person A—Pretends to be a teacher	Person B—Pretends to be a student
The teacher wants the student to sit down. First give an alpha command.	Student is walking around the room.
Example: "*John, you need to sit down.*"	Student sits down.
Next, give a beta command for the same task.	Student is walking around the room.
Example: "*How many times have I told you that you need to be in your chair when you are doing your assignment. Everyone else in the class remembers that expectation except you. I don't like to remind you time and time again what you need to be doing. You need to remember to work quietly while you are in your seat.*"	Student keeps walking around the room. At first he ignores the teacher and only eventually sits down.

Discuss the differences in teacher and student behavior you observed.

For example: The alpha command was clear and direct and the student complied right away. The beta command was long and showed teacher frustration. It took the student a long time to finally sit down. The student may have felt embarrassed being scolded in front of the entire class. The student was getting a lot of teacher attention for inappropriate behavior. This type of command could easily escalate into a power struggle between teacher and student.

127

Predictable Response Sequence

Having a well-thought-out and consistent procedure for all adults when dealing with students with challenging behaviors is the first step to getting a student back on the right track in a respectful and calm way. The procedure below is a specific predictable sequence of responses to inappropriate student behavior:

Scenario: Student is not following directions after the teacher gave clear directions and verbally acknowledged students doing the right thing.

1. Calmly tell the student what she should be doing.

2. Walk away calmly. Stay in vicinity of student and unobtrusively notice what happens.

3. If student makes an attempt to follow directions within ten seconds, tell student: "*You're making a good choice.*"

4. If student is still noncompliant after ten seconds, repeat your alpha command calmly and walk away.

5. If student makes an attempt to follow directions within the next ten seconds, tell student: "*You're making a good choice.*"

6. If student is still noncompliant after a further ten seconds, say calmly: "*You need to . . . or . . . .*" State a preplanned consequence (e.g., lose preferred activity, go to time out, stay after school). Walk away.

7. If student engages in dangerous behavior (e.g., throwing, hitting, kicking), see Chapter 14 (Responding to Escalating Behavior and Verbal Harassment).

In the above procedure, the teacher privately directs the student using an alpha command and then walks away, giving the student time to comply. If a student complies, the good choice must be reinforced immediately. Also notice that the teacher attempted two verbal corrections before applying a preplanned consequence for noncompliance. Figure 18 illustrates this sequence.

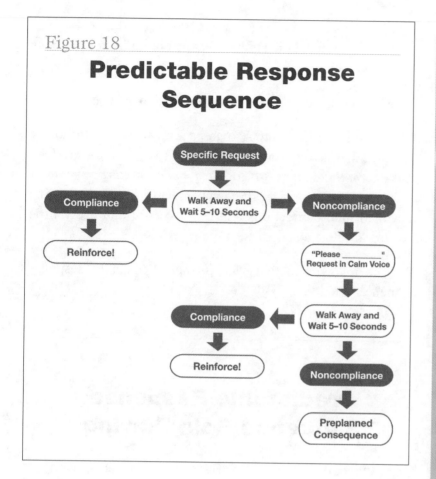

Figure 18

Predictable Response Sequence

Another example to illustrate this procedure:

1. Say: *"Please finish the problems on page 5."*

2. Walk away to give the student a few seconds to comply.

3. Deliver a brief warning that alerts the student to choose between displaying the expected behavior and earning positive consequences, or failing to comply and experiencing a penalty or loss of privilege. For example: *"You've been asked to complete problems on page 5. If you choose to do that, you can go out to recess with the class. If you choose not to work now, you need to stay in for recess later."*

4. If the student still doesn't comply, matter-of-factly deliver the penalty or loss of privilege.

While helping a student get back on track don't:

- Argue with the student.

- Hold a grudge.

- Try to make the student feel bad or guilty for previous poor choices.

Do acknowledge the desired behavior as soon as it occurs.

When the student attempts to go back to work, continuously reinforce by saying statements like, "*You made an excellent choice to continue your work*" or "*You made a mature choice to sit down and open your book.*" Remember that the student is being taught to follow directions and be successful and every little step toward that goal counts.

Try the following activity for further Predictable Response Sequence practice.

Activity

Predictable Response Sequence Role Playing

Practice the Predictable Response Sequence with another person. One person is the teacher, and the other person is the student.

First, the teacher gives the student a request (maybe the same as the above example). The student complies at the second request.

Next, the teacher gives the student the same request, but now the student doesn't comply.

chapter 13

Using Consequences to Change Group and Individual Behavior

Chapter Objectives:

○ Identify positive consequences to use in your classroom

○ Identify corrective consequences

○ Design integrated motivational systems to teach and reinforce positive behavior change

○ Teach on-task behavior (Concentration/Focus Power Game) during disruptions

Students will only learn to comply to classroom expectations and routines through direct teaching and *differential feedback* regarding the acceptability of their behavior. You must judiciously use positive and corrective consequences to make clear to the student the boundaries of acceptable and unacceptable behavior. For example, you may spend time clarifying "quiet voices" by having students demonstrate the right way to talk quietly.

Positive Consequences

Researchers are finding that positive reinforcement is a very powerful tool for behavior change (Maag, 2001). Positive consequences can be verbal or nonverbal (e.g., smile, wink, thumbs up, pat on shoulder, note) statements, privileges (e.g., seating choice, free time, trip to office), rewards (e.g., stickers, tangibles, edibles), and incentives (e.g., grades, token tickets, field trips). The only way to tell if a consequence is positive is if the behavior increases in the future.

Positive consequences always increase the likelihood of the behavior occurring. Corrective consequences, in contrast, decrease the likelihood of the behavior occurring. Observing student behavior provides information about whether a consequence is positive or corrective. If adults apply consequences believed to be corrective, but the student's inappropriate behavior does not change, the consequence may be reinforcing for the student and is therefore not effective. The following is an example of a fifth grade girl, Mieke. She performed at grade level and enjoyed being in the classroom. Each morning during independent math assignment, however, Mieke did not stay on task. She did not complete her assignments and had to stay in for recess to finish her work. When her behavior did not change after two weeks, the teacher talked with Mieke and asked what was going on. Mieke told the teacher that she did not like to go out to recess because some kids were bullying her. The teacher made an agreement that Mieke could stay in for recess if she got her math assignment completed. The teacher also made plans to deal with the bullying problem during recess.

The developmental and comfort level of students must always be considered when delivering reinforcement. While public praise at the elementary level may increase positive behavior for a particular student, it may be a punisher that decreases desired behavior for a secondary-level student. Hence, it is extremely important for educators to understand the developmental level and the individual preferences of their students. Reinforcement such as teacher praise, positive written or verbal feedback, acknowledgment, and encouragement are among the most readily available, easiest, and most natural forms of reinforcement. The following box lists examples of positive consequences.

Examples of Positive Consequences

- Sitting in teacher's chair

- Being first in line

- Leaving class two minutes early

- Free time

- Computer time

- Leading a lesson

- Additional time at recess

The school year should begin with clear, high behavioral expectations combined with frequent feedback and rewards for meeting those expectations. As the year progresses, the frequency of extrinsic rewards (e.g., tickets, tangibles) can decrease while the more natural (intrinsic) forms of reinforcement continue (e.g., academic and social success, teacher's verbal and/or written attention). This gradual change happens when the teacher observes students monitoring their own behavior as they become intrinsically motivated for doing the right thing.

At the beginning of the year, behavioral goals for the class should be reinforced frequently, depending on the performance level of the class, to shape the behaviors. As performance increases, the time between reward activities lengthens. A reinforcement system can be thinned to span a longer period of time. For example, at the beginning of the year, the class may earn a special activity each day for following directions the first time given. Then, a special activity may be earned twice a week, then once a week, and when students have mastered the skill, a new skill can be chosen and taught with a similar reinforcement schedule. Nevertheless, the teacher must intermittently provide specific verbal positive feedback until required skills are fluent. After a few weeks, the teacher may say: "*I just want to tell you how respectful this class is. Nearly every time I ask you to do something, you follow directions right away. It is great to be working with a neat class like this one.*" Goals must be clearly communicated to the students, and teachers must continually provide students with positive feedback when students meet

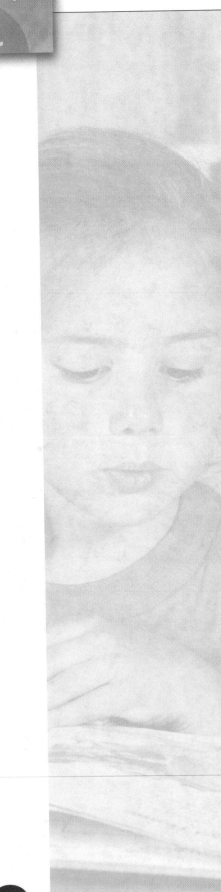

expectations. These systems can turn classroom behavior management into a positive experience for everyone.

Corrective Consequences

Researchers have found that the most effective feedback systems include both positive reinforcers for desired behavior and small corrective consequences for undesired behavior. It is important to remember, however, that systems based primarily on punishment result in unexpected consequences such as increased anger, vandalism, truancy, and drop out (Mayer, Butterworth, Nafpaktitis, & Sulzer-Azaroff, 1983).

A classroom system should include a continuum of rewards and consequences, from more natural and easily implemented forms, such as praise and corrective feedback (for example, if a student is running, the teacher might say: "*Stop. How are we supposed to move in the classroom?*" Response: "*We walk.*" Teacher: "*That's right, we walk. Show me.*") to more comprehensive and intensive forms that require more planning, such as token economies and level systems. The following box provides examples of corrective consequences.

Examples of Corrective Consequences

- Gentle verbal correction

- Loss of points or privileges

- Discussions

- Completion of self-report behavior form

- Removal into the hall or other time-out area

- Removal to the office

- Parent contact

- Isolation within the classroom

- Extra work

- Planned ignoring

Planned Ignoring

One consequence that is often effective for attention-getting behavior is planned ignoring. Planned ignoring is an active strategy to teach a student to behave in a more mature and responsible manner to earn attention. An effective teacher will never "tolerate" inappropriate behavior, but when planned ignoring is used as a consequence to misbehavior, the student is being told that some behaviors are not worthy of a response.

A gentle reprimand such as *"That's not OK. You need to sit down and open your book to page 5"* may precede ignoring, so that the student will know that the teacher is not condoning inappropriate behavior by ignoring it. The teacher should not only tell the student what he should not be doing, but also give specific instructions on what is expected at that moment so that the student has a chance to comply.

If classroom expectations are very clear and have been taught, and a student is still acting inappropriately to obtain teacher attention (e.g., talking out in class, getting up out of seat), the teacher may choose to ignore the behavior and provide positive feedback to students who are following directions. For example: *"John, I see that you have your book open to page 5. Sally, you have started on the problems on page 5."* As soon as the target student is complying, provide reassuring feedback. *"You made a good choice opening your book to page 5."* The teacher also needs to be proactive and catch the student doing the right thing before inappropriate behavior occurs.

A teacher can never ignore behavior that involves hurting other students or him/herself, or when more than one student is involved in the inappropriate behavior. Rather than escalating the situation by trying to figure out what is going on, provide short, clear directions for what the students should do. For example: *"John, go to your desk and work on the puzzle. Tom, get the poetry book from my desk, go to your table, and look at the book for a few minutes."*

Classwide Motivational Systems

Successful motivation systems are built on effective consequences. As with real situations, schools must provide consequences, rewards, or incentives for desired behavior and small corrective consequences or aversives for undesired behavior. Careful planning is required to choose rewards that actually increase positive behavior and decrease problem behavior. The consequences must be ones that teachers will use consistently. The most effective systems use positive consequences liberally and corrective consequences sparingly.

In effective classroom-management systems, a teacher should use a combination of group contingencies and individual contingencies. After teaching students classroom expectations and the behaviors needed to meet those expectations, the teacher must design a system to provide feedback to students regarding their success or failure at meeting those expectations.

You must be very clear about which situations you can resolve in your classroom and which behaviors need to be referred to the administrator. The ability to teach appropriate behavior in the classroom through incentives and consequences takes time and effort, but the benefits to the students can often be greater than more severe punishments such as suspension or expulsion.

The Green/Red Card Game

Here we provide you with an example of a classwide motivational technique, the Green/Red Card Game. This game has been very effective with students of all ages as well as adults. A superintendent in Manitoba, Canada, used a Green/Red Card Game to keep his staff from having side conversations during staff meetings. The rule was: "If there are no side conversations during the meeting, the card stays on green, and you will get to leave at 3:45, 15 minutes before official dismissal time. I will turn the card to red if I hear side conversations, and you will have to stay until 4:00."

The game can be adjusted to the motivational and developmentally appropriate needs of your students. There are several rationales for the Green/Red Card Game:

- Students need to know whether or not they are meeting expectations.

- An external system like this helps students develop an internal self-management system.

- It promotes teamwork and shared responsibility for the success of all team members.

How to Create a Green/Red Card Game

1. Make an 8" x 11" card (laminating optional), green on one side and red on the other.

2. Place the card so the class can see it (e.g., on a string hanging from the chalkboard or on an easel with chart paper).

3. Draw two boxes to mark points where students can see them (e.g., on chalkboard, chart paper). Title the boxes "Green" and "Red."

4. Have an intermittent audible signal such as a computer prompter program and a timer or stopwatch.

5. Tell students the following:

   When the whole class is following directions and showing respect, the card will be on Green. If someone is not following directions, I will turn the card to Red. As soon as everyone is following directions, the card will go back to Green.

   Once in a while, the beeper will beep and you will get a point. If the beeper beeps when the card is on Green, you will get a point on the green side. If the beeper beeps when the card is on Red, you will get a point on the Red side.

   If at the end of the period you have more points on Green, you will get to move up one space on the chart. When we get to the top, there will be a surprise for the class.

While using this technique, reinforce students for following directions, being responsible, and showing respect.

At the end of the period, tally marks and fill in space on a chart or object (e.g., see the **Rocket, Thermometer**, **Map**, and **Target** reproducibles for ideas). This game has also been very effective in teaching self-monitoring to individual older students.

We are fast, quiet, and careful!

We're on Target!

Reaching our goal,
state by state!

chapter thirteen • *Best Behavior*

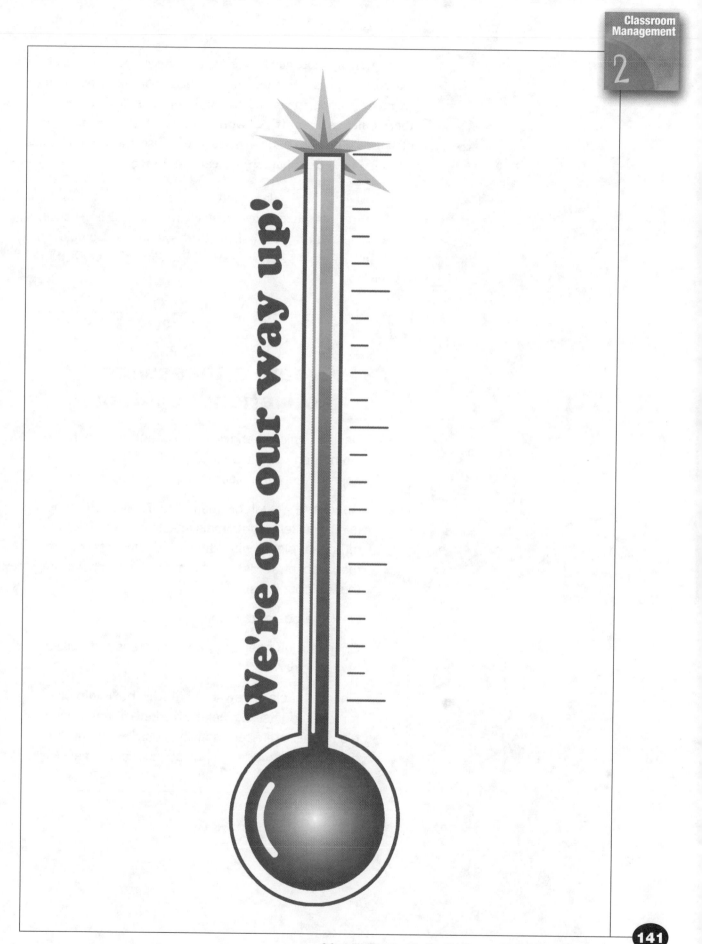

We're on our way up!

Class performance may be graphed after each period on a chart placed in a prominent location in the classroom. Charts come in many forms, including thematic designs such as rockets, thermometers, countries, words, parts of the brain, names of bones, muscles, plants, insects, etc. Use the reproducibles provided with this chapter or create your own.

Some teachers have taken pictures of the entire class and cut the picture into puzzle pieces. Each time a goal is reached, a piece is added until the whole picture is complete. Complete the following activity as a start to creating a classwide motivational system.

Activity

Create a Classwide Motivational System

1. Decide which behavior you want to teach or strengthen (e.g., working quietly, asking for help appropriately, transitions).

2. Choose a visual or theme to record progress (e.g., basketball, animals, skeleton with names of bones, plants with Latin words, insects, or the map, rocket, target, or thermometer as shown in the reproducibles).

3. Design a poster to record progress.

4. Choose a number of spaces or areas until class reward is earned.

5. Choose a class reward that will be reinforcing for all students (e.g., extra basketball time, early dismissal, preferred activity such as computer time or silent reading, special guest or animal).

Concentration/Focus Power Game

This strategy is an inoculation against the spread of disruptive behavior. It helps students stay on task while there are disruptions in the classroom. In this game, you challenge students to be able to work for a long period of time and ignore you while you are trying to interrupt them. The game is ideal for elementary and middle school students. At the high school level, ignoring should be explained and modeled in a similar way, and students who successfully ignore distractions in class should be immediately rewarded. Students need to practice ignoring distractions under controlled situations so that when a difficult situation arises, they go into "autopilot" and know exactly what to do. They will also know through experience that they will be rewarded for "playing the game" correctly, which increases their motivation to ignore inappropriate behavior when it occurs. The following box outlines the basic steps of the Concentration/Focus Power Game.

Basic Steps of the Concentration/Focus Power Game

- Make a chart to record the time.

- Set a goal (number of minutes).

- Tell students you want to teach them to concentrate and focus in spite of minor distractions.

- Tell them the rules of the game. Say: *"I will try to distract you but you can't look up, smile, or talk until I say 'stop.'"*

- You should be the only person trying to distract students.

- Use a stopwatch to keep track of the time and to look official.

- Model with examples and nonexamples.

- Practice for a short period in the beginning.

- Focus only on students who are doing well.

- If a few students are not concentrating, simply say: *"Stop. Some of you did a great job. We'll try again some other time."*

Mark the time on the chart. When students are doing well after a few trials, tell them that there may be occasions when someone doesn't make a good choice and tries to interrupt their work. You will then ask them to play the Concentration/Focus Power Game, keeping in mind that they will never know when they will get a reward. For example, if the group has done a great job concentrating and not getting distracted, you may say: *"That was great. Let's go outside and take ten minutes of extra break time."* At other times you may simply thank the students for doing a great job. Students should not expect a reward each time they play the Concentration/Focus Power Game.

Progress monitoring has been shown to be an effective motivational tool. A visual picture of progress can be a reward in itself (see the two reproducible examples). Students can earn a class reward when they have reached a predetermined goal.

Play the game when all students are doing well. Make sure the teacher is the only person who plays the "distracter." Don't give the message that you only do this when someone is misbehaving.

To conclude this chapter, please take a few minutes to reflect on the following questions.

Reflection

Changing Group and Individual Behavior

1. What would you do if two or three students in a class of 30 constantly disrupted the class?

2. What are some strategies you would use to keep all students on task during independent work?

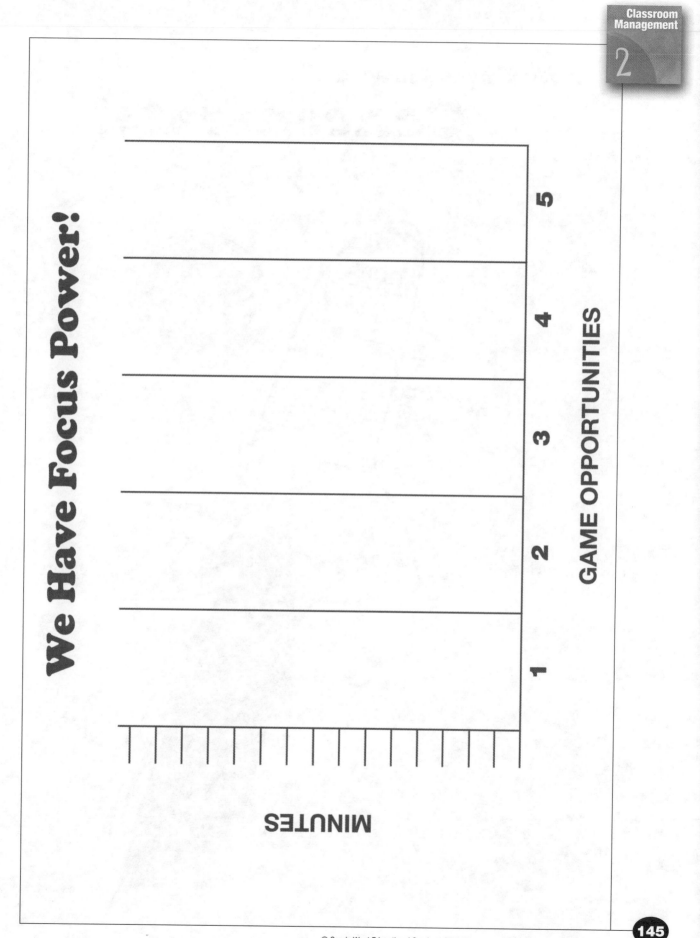

We Have Focus Power!

MINUTES

GAME OPPORTUNITIES

1 2 3 4 5

145

We Know How to ...
Concentrate!

chapter thirteen • *Best Behavior*

Schoolwide
Classroom Management
1 2
4 3
Family Support
Individual Student Supports

Individual Student Supports

chapter 14

Responding to Escalating Behavior and Verbal Harassment

Chapter Objectives:

- ○ Identify common assumptions that get teachers into power struggles

- ○ Identify the phases of behavioral escalation

- ○ Learn procedures to prevent escalating behavior

- ○ Learn procedures to de-escalate behaviors and restore the environment

Escalating behavior and verbal harassment exhibited by students seriously undermines proper functioning of a school and classroom. Behaviors such as aggression, severe disruption, and acting-out can cause major problems for adults and students in terms of personal safety and stress, as well significantly disrupt the teaching and learning processes in school. There is no question that teachers need to develop and implement safe and effective plans for managing escalating behavior. In this chapter, we will identify common assumptions

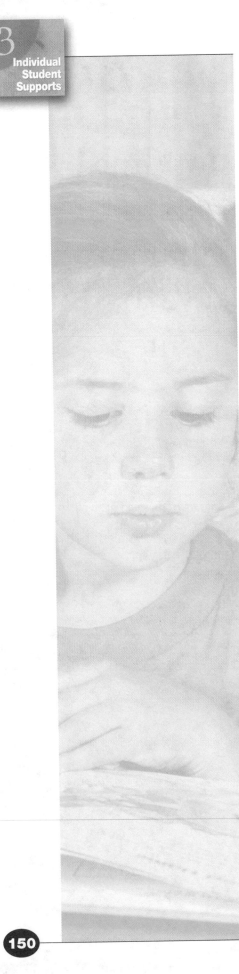

that lead teachers into power struggles and offer procedures to de-escalate behaviors. If the escalating behaviors persist, the function of the behavior must be examined and a positive behavior support plan to reduce escalating behaviors must be developed and implemented. In this chapter and in Chapter 15 we will provide you with tools to accomplish these outcomes.

The Challenge of Escalating Behavior

The behavior support techniques that work with typical students may not work for students exhibiting more severe behavior problems, especially those who are prone to escalation. In fact, some of these practices may make conditions worse, especially with students whose problem behavior tends to be explosive and sudden. It is important to address the behavior without causing the behavior to escalate. This can be quite a balancing act.

Students who act out repeatedly may not have strategies for identifying sources of the problem, generating options, evaluating their options, negotiating with others, and acting on their plans. Such strategies need to be systematically and directly taught. Like everyone else, students with severe problem behavior need to be successful and gain a sense of competence. They will be responsive if appropriate goals can be established that they are likely to meet.

In general, these students do not experience academic or social success in school, and often their behavior can be brought under control if a teacher can interrupt the behavior chain that leads to escalation early in the phase. This does not mean we have to appease; it means effectively responding to students so they learn to manage their own behavior. To begin, reflect on the following scenario and how you would handle it.

Reflection

How Would You Respond?

Louis is in a regular classroom but is not eligible for special education services. He is a disruptive student and has a long history of arguing with teachers, shouting out, throwing books onto the floor, and tearing papers angrily. He rarely stays on task when given assignments. At the moment, Louis is arguing with you. How would you handle this situation?

Dealing With Escalating Behavior: Assumptions

Often, adults respond to escalating behaviors in a manner that makes the problem worse. Some of us may be operating from the following assumptions. Each of these assumptions can drive behaviors that we may regret later:

- I can't let a student get away with this. What will the other students think?

- I need to establish authority.

- I need to settle down agitated students.

- I need to be in control.

Phases of Behavioral Escalation

Rapidly escalating behavior is a common pattern for children and youth with chronic problem behavior. Becoming familiar with the phases of the acting-out cycle can help you to understand the behavioral processes and common behavioral indicators characterizing each phase. Colvin (1999) and Walker et al., (1995) have illustrated a seven-phase cycle describing the constellation of behaviors that make up escalating behavior sequences. The phases of the escalation cycle are based on the intensity and order of appearance of the behaviors. Figure 19 provides a graphic illustration of the

phases of escalating behavior. We will review in detail each of the phases, including behavioral indicators.

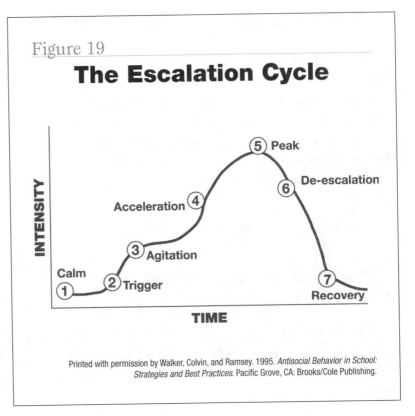

Figure 19

The Escalation Cycle

Printed with permission by Walker, Colvin, and Ramsey. 1995. *Antisocial Behavior in School: Strategies and Best Practices.* Pacific Grove, CA: Brooks/Cole Publishing.

Phase 1: Calm

During this phase, students demonstrate appropriate behavior and are generally cooperative and responsive to teacher directions. The student may engage and participate in classroom activities for an extended period of time, follow rules and expectations, be responsive to feedback, and occasionally initiate appropriate behavior toward others. The student is often ignored during this phase, because the adults are taking advantage of this respite from acting-out. This is a good time to establish behavior goals and provide consistent positive feedback for appropriate behavior.

Phase 2: Trigger

Triggers are any activity, event, or behavior that sets off the escalating phases of the acting-out behavior cycle. Some triggers may be present continuously but only have an effect in conjunction with some specific event or action.

School-based triggers include conflicts resulting from ineffective communication or miscommunication with others in school. Students exhibiting acting-out behavior often misperceive the actions of others and think they are being treated negatively or unfairly when they are not. Changes in routines, provocation by peers, ineffective problem solving, ill-timed correction of their errors, or a simple teacher request/demand may set off a student and start the escalation cycle.

Non-school-based triggers or setting events include home and social conditions such as poverty, unemployment, abuse, neglect, poor adult modeling of appropriate behavior, negative neighborhood influences, sleep deprivation, inadequate diet, or medical conditions. These factors may play a role in making it more difficult for a student to make appropriate choices. Classroom teachers have limited influence over these external factors (Walker et al., 1995), so it is important to keep a focus on the here and now. When the student has not been taught how to respond effectively to the trigger, he or she may become more agitated (Phase 3), and the behavior may escalate (Phase 4) rapidly.

Phase 3: Agitation

Students who do not effectively manage Phase 2 triggers are likely to exhibit agitated behavior. This phase is characterized by emotional responses: anger, withdrawal, worry, anxiety, or frustration. Students' eyes may dart about from here to there, with little focus. It becomes difficult for them to continue conversations. Agitated students often increase their hand movements—drumming their fingers, tapping their pencils, opening and closing their books, and/or mumbling under their breath. They move in and out of groups, vacillate between off-task and on-task behavior, and have difficulty attending to academic tasks (Colvin, 1999). Some students like to be left alone, becoming quiet or withdrawing from group activities.

Phase 4: Acceleration

Students in this phase exhibit escalated behaviors that are likely to dominate the teacher's attention or even cause alarm. They question, argue, and engage in confrontational interactions; they are defiant of teacher demands and expectations, often engaging in off-task behavior. Many students provoke others, and may use offensive language or destroy property

during this phase. They may demonstrate compliance but still behave inappropriately. Colvin (1999) calls this "limit-testing." A student may work on an assigned task but also act out, or comply with a demand but only partially, or comply at a lower than expected level. For example, the teacher asks the student to complete the entire math section, but the student does only half of it. The student starts whining and wants to escape from classroom activities. When the teacher asks for the completed assignment, the student makes threats. Such threats may pose a danger and should not be ignored.

Phase 5: Peak

The peak phase is the most dangerous and disruptive to the class. In this phase, students with acting-out behavior may well be a threat to themselves or others. They may engage in serious destruction of property, physical assault, or self-directed negative behavior such as physically hurting themselves, hyperventilation, or severe tantrums. Behavior during this phase is out of control. Any discussion with the student during this time is unproductive. When a student is at the peak of escalation, it should be treated as an emergency. We will outline appropriate procedures later in the chapter.

During the escalation and peak phases, the teacher must secure the safety of all students, even if it means having all students except the student with escalating behavior leave the classroom quickly.

Finally, after the incident, the student will de-escalate and may display the characteristics listed under Phase 6.

Phase 6: De-Escalation

This phase is characterized by student disengagement and reduced acting-out behavior. Students show confusion by wandering around, staring at the floor, fidgeting, or just sitting or standing. Some students may want to apologize for their behavior; others want to withdraw or even sleep after the incident. Some deny their behavior or blame others for the incident.

Phase 7: Recovery

Recovery is the final phase of Colvin's (1999) behavior cycle, during which the student returns to a normal state. Gradually, the disengaged student begins to respond to teacher instruction, often preferring mechanical or routine tasks that are easy to perform. They generally want to avoid discussing the incident and are not ready for difficult tasks requiring teacher assistance or having to cooperate with peers.

Not every student engaging in acting-out behavior progresses through every phase of the acting-out cycle at the same rate. Nevertheless, school staff should be able to identify behavioral signs and be prepared to intervene as appropriately as possible to minimize the risk that a student will reach peak phase and its potential dangers. In the next section we provide strategies for intervening at each phase of the acting-out cycle.

Basic Approaches to Preventing Escalating Behavior

Specific strategies and interventions have been developed to manage each of the seven phases of Colvin's acting-out cycle. Managing a student's acting-out behavior during the earlier phases of the cycle may prevent the occurrence of more serious and destructive behavior in the later phases. The emphasis during the first phase (calm) is on teaching acceptable behavior and providing the student with lots of positive feedback. If the problem behavior has been reoccurring, the teacher must find out what triggers the behavior and provide the student with strategies to deal with the trigger. Sometimes it is very difficult to find the trigger. Classroom interactions may need to be videotaped for several days and analyzed. A staff member other than the teacher may need to conduct an Antecedent, Behavior, Consequence (ABC) observation. Consider the following true example.

Tes, a ten-year-old girl, was, along with her younger sister, removed from her parents at age five after both girls had experienced severe neglect and sexual abuse. After living in several foster homes, the girls were adopted by two different families. Tes was placed in a special education classroom at age eight. Her academic skills were low, and she displayed frequent incidents

of violent and destructive behavior in an inconsistent manner. It seemed like her outbursts would come "out of the blue." Some days she would be totally appropriate and at other times, while performing similar tasks, she would suddenly throw her books, tear papers, swear loudly, and throw her chair and desk. After examining hours of classroom tapes, the only trigger the staff could identify was when Tes slid down in her chair, she would escalate quickly to a major blow-up that was unsafe for her and for the entire class.

The teacher made a large sign, "I am calm and good at what I do," and posted it in the front of the room. During a calm phase, she asked Tes to read the sign and told her: "I want to help you to make good choices when you are having a difficult time in class. Sometimes I may ask you to read the sign. You can read the sign as often as you need to calm yourself down." Tes smiled and agreed to try.

The next time she slouched in her chair, the teacher asked her to read the sign. She threw her book and yelled, "I'm calm and good at what I do!" She proceeded to yell the phrase while demolishing her papers with a pencil. The teacher carefully herded the other students in the group to another part of the classroom and ignored Tes's challenge. Soon Tes was copying the phrase and wrote: "I am clam and god at what I do."

When she had de-escalated, her teacher told her: "You did an excellent job of calming yourself down. How about if the next time, I ask you to go to your desk and calm yourself down?" Tes agreed. During the next few weeks, she had several opportunities to practice her new skill, and each time she became calmer more quickly. After about one month, she was able to attend classes in the regular classroom, where the teachers posted the same sign and gave her a cue to look at the sign when she triggered.

Slouching in the chair was probably not the real trigger, but it was the only behavior that signaled a full-blown escalation. Even though her teacher worked closely with the adoptive mother, she didn't learn until several years later that all along Tes had been stealing food and hiding it. In retrospect, the trigger may have been inadequate nutrition. Her adoptive mother punished her by allowing her to eat only certain amounts and types of food at certain times of the day, which may not have been enough for this extremely fast-growing child. Hunger may have irritated her. The teacher didn't have control over the home situation but still had to teach Tes to deal with the triggers nonviolently and in a socially accepted way. The strategy worked well for her. Tes has been in a successful marriage for several years, has one son, and is "Calm and happy and good at what she does!"

As this example illustrates, it is most important to identify a trigger and interrupt the escalation cycle of a student who demonstrates extreme behaviors. If no trigger can be identified, the teacher must be aware of the agitation and escalation phases and try to divert the behavior from escalating through behavior management and teaching. A teacher can quickly escalate the behavior by engaging in a power struggle, getting into the student's face, scolding the student in front of peers, or touching the student. These tactics must be avoided at all times. The teacher must give clear and short directions on what the student needs to do (see the Predictable Response Sequence in Chapter 12), use a neutral, businesslike tone, and remain respectful with the student.

Basic Approaches to De-Escalating Behaviors and Restoring the Environment

Strategies for managing behavior in the last three phases—peak, de-escalation, and recovery—concentrate on maintaining safety for all students, managing crises, promoting re-entry behavior, and conducting follow-up. In the remainder of this chapter, we present procedures to prevent and manage escalating behavior. Several considerations should be kept in mind:

1. **Consideration 1: Escalating behavior is a phase in a chain of problem behavior.** Typically, escalating behavior does not occur in isolation ("All of a sudden we have a serious incident on our hands."). Rather, there is an identifiable behavior chain in which escalating behavior is one part of the chain, and, most importantly, it occurs later in the chain.

2. **Consideration 2: Intervening early in the behavioral chain can disrupt the whole chain.** Given that escalating behavior occurs later in the behavioral

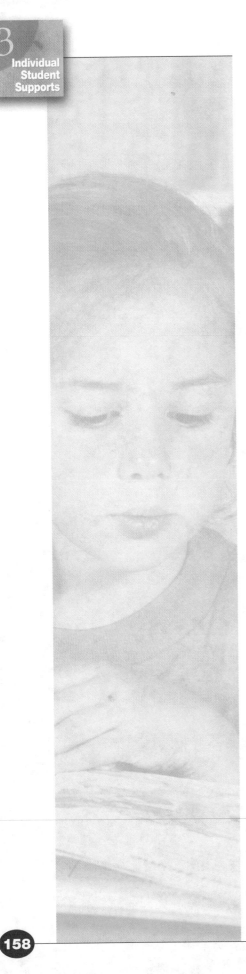

chain, strategies can be used to target behaviors early in the chain. In this way the chain is altered and subsequent behaviors in the chain are prevented from occurring.

3. **Consideration 3: The surest method for preventing escalating behavior is to provide a strong focus on school success.** When students succeed at school academically, socially, or through successful participation in school activities such as drama, music, clubs, and sports, there is much less chance they will engage in the behavioral chain leading to escalating behavior.

4. **Consideration 4: Escalating-behavior management plans need to be part of a proactive school-wide discipline plan.** It has been well established that school faculties that systematically work hard together to establish a strong, positive school climate have less serious problem behavior. In these schools, staff use a continuum of procedures to directly teach and maintain expected behavior and to address and correct problem behavior. Escalating-behavior management becomes part of the continuum for addressing problem behavior.

Critical Components of a Comprehensive Intervention Plan

The comprehensive intervention plan for managing escalating behavior can be divided into four stages or classes: (1) prevention, (2) interruption, (3) response, and (4) follow-up.

Initially, the student may be productively or satisfactorily engaged in the class or school activities. In this stage, strategies are designed to maintain the student and essentially *prevent* escalating behavior. If events or triggers unsettle the student, giving rise to the beginnings of problem behavior, strategies are designed to *interrupt* the behavior pattern, in other words, to catch the problems early and redirect the student to engage in the present class activities. The third intervention stage involves what we typically refer to as *respond*. The behavioral chain is going to run its course, and the student exhibits serious behavior escalation. The intent of these strategies is safety—to minimize

the likelihood of anyone getting hurt and to minimize the level of disruption to the class or school activity. The final component addresses the period following an incident or following the prevention of an incident. At this point the emphasis is on *follow-up*, in which staff debrief the situation and develop or modify plans accordingly. It is extremely important at this stage that the student (and the adult) is calm and positively engaged in a directed activity. The student should understand that adult attention is given when behavior is appropriate.

Best-practice strategies are now presented for each of these intervention classes. Table 2 provides a summary of the cycle, including behavioral indicators and indicated responses.

Phases, Behaviors, and
Interventions of the Escalation Cycle

Phase	Behavioral Indicator	Intervention Class	Strategy
Calm	• Able to follow directions • Less likely to react to provoking situations • Responsive to praise and other forms of reinforcement • Able to make mistakes and receive correction • Interested in showing work and telling about accomplishments	Prevention	• Conduct functional assessment • Identify alternative behaviors to teach • Utilize preventive techniques
Trigger	• Provocation from another person • Interruption of routine/reward • Problem-solving situations • Continued errors • Having to face consequences for behavior	Prevention	• Identify the antecedent/trigger • Modify the influence of the antecedent • Prompt alternative behaviors • Teach a problem-solving routine
Agitation	• Increased body/eye/hand movement • Cryptic speech/no speech	Interruption	• Provide quiet and alone time • Make easier work available • Provide concrete task or response options
Acceleration	• Engagement behaviors (questioning, arguing, provoking) to get predictable response • Threats, intimidation, defiance • Leaves situation • Physical aggression • Self-abuse • Property destruction	Response	• Intervene early in the chain • Rehearse expected behaviors • Provide reminders • Modify the task or task demands • Alter the physical arrangement • Withdraw from the individual • Teach a different routine for meeting the function of the behavior • Prompt the new routine • Praise engagement on the new routine
Peak	• Physical aggression • Self-abuse • Property destruction • Tantrums • Hyperventilation	Response	• Physically restrain the student (as allowed by your district) • Clear the room • Give a time out • Get emergency assistance
De-Escalation	• Confusion • Attempts to reconcile • Withdrawal behaviors • Responsive to concrete directions • Denial of serious incident	Follow-up	• Praise return to normal activities • Debrief if appropriate
Recovery	• Willingness to resume routine, especially tasks that do not require interaction • Subdued behavior • Reluctance to talk about/denial of behavior	Follow-up	• Focus on normal routine • Praise appropriate behavior • Rehearse problem-solving routine

Class 1: Prevention

The intent of all of these practices is to increase the likelihood that the student will be productively and successfully engaged in the class and school activities. In this way, appropriate behavior may be maximized and inappropriate behavior minimized. As we have discussed throughout this book, it is critical that the school as a whole and the classroom are positive, predictable environments with clear expectations. A schoolwide social skills curriculum must be taught that focuses on effective problem solving, anger management, impulse control, and empathy (e.g., the Second Step program). The social skills must be practiced by students and reinforced daily by all staff members. In addition, the physical design of the classroom needs to be carefully considered (Colvin, 2002; Colvin & Lazar, 1997). Careful planning of classroom organization and scheduling is essential, and appropriate academic placement of students will maximize their chances for success.

Class 2: Interruption

In this stage, strategies are designed to catch the problem behaviors at their onset, that is, to interrupt the behavioral chain so that the problem behaviors do not worsen or escalate. The teacher can defuse the student when a problem behavior is likely to occur. For example, Johnny spends Wednesdays with his verbally abusive father. Every Wednesday afternoon he becomes more and more agitated and usually escalates just before school is out. The teacher could talk to Johnny and acknowledge that it must be difficult to go home with Dad and ask if Johnny would like to spend time on the computer the last hour of school on Wednesdays. If Johnny leaves school in a calm manner, he can probably better tolerate some of his father's inconsiderate words. Depending on his age, he can be taught assertive and calm responses to his father's behavior.

Additional examples of managing escalating behavior can be seen in a video program featuring Geoff Colvin titled, *Defusing Anger and Aggression* (1999). The video provides examples and solutions for behavior that is off-task, challenging, confrontational, defiant, disrespectful, or intimidating. In addition, it deals with behavior characterized by agitation, depression, and avoidance.

161

Class 3: Crisis Response

When the student's behavior has reached levels where the personal safety of staff, students, and the involved student becomes a serious concern, strategies are designed for "safety first." A plan must be in place to respond to a crisis situation. During a calm time, all students must be taught "room clear" procedures. These procedures should be practiced on a regular basis just like a fire drill. During a room clear, all students except the escalating student quickly and in orderly fashion leave the room and go to a safe place (e.g., library, cafeteria, playground). The escalated student stays in the room with supervision until he/she de-escalates or help arrives. Help procedures on how and who to call (e.g., principal, crisis response team, security, police) must be clearly defined and easily available. In addition, legal requirements or school district mandates on safety must be followed.

Class 4: Follow-Up

Follow-up is needed if the student displays crisis behavior and if this behavior is prevented or avoided. The intent is to review the situation, identify triggers, evaluate responses, and make provision in the planning for future events. The team must decide if Functional Behavioral Assessment (FBA) and Behavior Intervention Plan (BIP) modifications are needed and who will be responsible. An excellent resource for conducting a functional assessment and developing BIPs is the book *Why Johnny Doesn't Behave: Twenty Tips for Measurable BIPs* (Bateman & Golly, 2003). A debriefing with the student and perhaps the parents might be necessary. When meeting with the student alone, ask what would help him/her to avoid a similar situation in the future.

Techniques for Managing Agitation

Our colleague Geoff Colvin (1999) offers an excellent strategy for responding to escalation and provides a step-by-step approach to responding to student behavior that defuses, rather than escalates, the behavior. Figure 20 summarizes his general approach. We recommend that you review Colvin's material in detail and remember that your response to escalation will be unique to each student. If you are to become skilled at responding to escalating behavior patterns, you will need to study this material extensively, be aware of assumptions you may hold that interfere with a calm, businesslike approach, and acknowledge that your behavior often will be the difference between a dangerous, disruptive escalation and a return to expected school and classroom routines. The choice is yours!

Figure 20

Colvin's Approach to Defusing Escalation

If a student shows signs of escalation:

- Stop and think.

- Restate the expected behavior and bring other students on task.

- Recognize other students for acceptable behavior.

- Speak privately, and acknowledge agitation calmly.

- Isolate, ignore, or offer support to the escalating student.

- Give the student a positive choice (e.g., "You can either get back to work or go to the office.").

- Step away and give the student time to respond ("I will give you a chance to think about it."), unless it is an emergency.

- If the student complies, recognize and acknowledge cooperation.

- If the student continues to escalate, implement the preplanned consequence or school emergency procedures as appropriate (e.g., room clear, get other adults).

Printed with permission by Walker, Colvin, and Ramsey. 1995. *Antisocial Behavior in Schools: Strategies and Best Practices.* Pacific Grove, CA: Brooks/Cole Publishing.

---

chapter 15

Thinking Functionally About Behavior

Chapter Objectives:

○ Define Functional Behavioral Assessment (FBA)

○ List the outcomes of a complete FBA

○ Discuss methods for conducting an FBA

○ Describe information needed for an FBA

We have examined a variety of ways to organize your school and classroom to prevent problem behaviors. You have also seen that for some children, even the best preventive strategies will not work at all times. We will now begin to explore ways to support the children who challenge our resources and skills.

Benefits of Functional Behavioral Assessment

Some traditional behavior management strategies, such as punishment or simple reinforcement, are not effective in changing chronic and intractable behavior problems *if they are not logically linked to the causes and functions of*

the behavior(s). For example, if José is using noncompliance to get out of completing a seatwork task, sending him to a time out will not change the behavior because he is getting out of doing the work anyway! A better method for José might be to ignore the minor noncompliance and tell him that he will not be allowed to go to lunch until the seatwork is finished. We also would make sure the seatwork task is of appropriate difficulty and interesting, and perhaps offer a positive consequence for acceptable work.

A process called Functional Behavioral Assessment (FBA) can be helpful in developing effective and positive behavior support plans (O'Neill et al., 1997; Crone & Horner, 2003). Effective positive behavior support plans include adapting the curriculum, instruction, and environment to individual student needs. Instruction is defined as how you teach, curriculum is defined as what you teach, and environment is defined as the physical environment where you teach.

In this chapter you will learn how to use FBA to define problem behavior(s) and the consequences that maintain them. We will also learn to use our functional assessment information to develop behavior support plans. Thinking functionally about the problem behaviors we encounter gives a simple road map to developing effective support plans that are logically linked to the reason(s) students misbehave.

In order to get you thinking about a problem you would like to assess and solve, use the following space to briefly reflect on a student of yours with problem behaviors.

Thinking Functionally About Behavior

Student's First Name: _____

Grade: _____

Problem behaviors you see:

Places and times where the behaviors are likely to occur:

What would you like the student to be doing instead of the problem behaviors?

What Is Functional Behavioral Assessment (FBA)?

FBA is a process of identifying the events that predict and maintain patterns of problem behavior. Federal special education law specifies the use of a "functional behavioral assessment" in a specific manner, to be used to determine if a behavior is a manifestation of a student's disability. In this chapter we will not detail these procedures. We use functional behavior assessment procedures to *think functionally about behavior*.

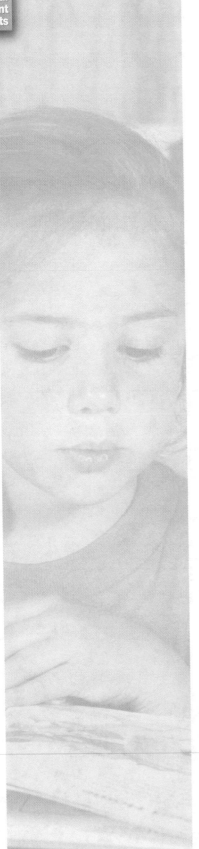

When we think functionally about behavior, we don't look for the source of the problem in the student's disability or home life (e.g., the student is "hyperactive" or "he acts that way because his parents are not helping at home"); rather, we look at those factors that we can control in the school environment (instruction, curriculum, and environment). We try to figure out what the student is getting (e.g., attention and/or avoidance) when he/she misbehaves.

What Are the Outcomes of a Functional Behavioral Assessment?

In order to think functionally about behavior and to make a logical and effective response to student support, you need to achieve four critical outcomes from a functional behavioral assessment. While the process may look simple, it can be increasingly challenging depending on the presenting problem. The key outcomes of an FBA are:

1. Clearly defining the challenging behavior(s).

2. Identifying the events, times, and situations when the behaviors occur.

3. Identifying the consequences that maintain the behaviors.

4. Developing a summary statement about the "function" of the problem behaviors.

FBA involves collecting information in order to make statements about what sets off the behavior and what consequences are maintaining them. In other words, what makes the behavior "work" for the student? Following are examples of correct functional assessment summary statements: Jenny, age 11, talks out in Mrs. Jones's science class in order to gain peer attention. Fred, age 13, is late to Mr. Smith's math class because he avoids work that is too difficult. Melissa, age 8, pushes and kicks peers on the playground in order to escape other peers who are teasing her. José, age 16, makes off-color jokes in class to gain attention from his peers. Pierre, age 17, uses inappropriate language during science class to get adult and peer attention and to avoid doing the work that is boring to him.

Incorrect examples of functional assessment summary statements would be: Jenny talks out in Mrs. Jones's class because she is unable to control herself; Fred is late to Mr. Smith's class because he doesn't care about schoolwork; and Melissa pushes and kicks peers on the playground because she lacks anger management skills. While there may be some truth to these statements, they are not statements about the *function of the challenging behaviors* (why it works for the student), nor is it possible to test whether these statements are true.

When Should You Conduct an FBA?

Designing an individualized behavior support plan can be time consuming and will require regular adjustments and data collection to support decision making and be effective (see Chapter 16 for more details). Because of the time demands, you should reserve functional assessments for those students in your class who are not responding to your classroom management systems.

We recommend that a range of classroom management and group interventions (such as the Green/Red Card Game described in Chapter 13) be implemented to reduce the problem behavior before beginning FBA. When a student is chronically referred to the office for behavior problems, however, a Functional Behavioral Assessment is indicated to build an effective support plan. A final observation: Functional assessment results will not remain stable for long and will need to be conducted at regular intervals during ongoing implementation of a behavior support plan.

The FBA Is a Continuous Process

Functional Behavioral Assessment should be the central component of your behavior support planning. This means that the FBA is a continuous process. Sometimes, when behavior support plans solve one problem, they may create new problems. These new problems may involve the use of limited resources (e.g., teacher time, incentives, and materials). By continuing the FBA process, you will be gathering information in order to make decisions about the efficiency and effective-

ness of the plan. For example, a behavior support plan that rewards a student with computer time after completion of a class assignment may create behavior management problems in the classroom. If there are a limited number of computers, other students may develop resentment, or use of the computer may not serve as a reward for the desired behavior for a long period of time, or the teacher may find she is spending too much time providing computer instruction instead of working with other students.

Functional assessment allows collection of information that is linked directly to the development of behavior support plans. The information collected is used to develop support plans; FBA is not for diagnostic labeling. Educators find it useful because assistance for problems is not driven by eligibility for special education. Instead, assistance is provided based on need.

Functional assessment not only helps in the development of effective and efficient support plans, but it also helps us avoid programmatic errors. The danger of making problem behavior worse is very real. We have all seen instances of children having tantrums to gain a treat or children who behave aggressively to avoid a task and are then sent to the corner for their behavior. In each case, the presumed solution actually reinforced the problem behavior.

Conducting a Functional Behavioral Assessment

There are three major methods for conducting a functional assessment: (1) interviews, (2) direct observation of the student, and (3) testing a hypothesis. An example of the last method would be, if you think a student is acting out to gain attention, to try ignoring the student when he is engaged in minor inappropriate behaviors that do not hurt himself or others. We do *not* recommend this practice except with expert supervision and, for this reason, recommend only interviews and direct observation for classroom use. We have found that conducting a Functional Behavioral Assessment interview is an efficient and effective method for most students. We also recommend that you confirm your interview findings with direct observation of the student. This simple tool will help you identify the major information needed to complete a functional assessment and build a support plan.

FBA Interview

The FBA interview was designed to allow teachers to view problem behavior from a functional perspective. A functional perspective examines what environmental features may be maintaining the problem behavior. Moreover, it allows teachers to identify predictors of problems that are most likely to occur, thus allowing teachers to target limited resources in a more efficient manner. The following items are components of this interview:

Student Name, Grade, Date, and Staff Reporting: Each of these items is useful for record keeping.

Student Profile: We have found that it is important to ask teachers to list strengths or positive attributes of the student. Focusing only on negative behavior is counterproductive.

Antecedents (Triggers) and Setting Events: Antecedents also shed light on when the behavior does and does not occur. For example, an antecedent for talking back to the teacher may be a directive given by a teacher in a harsh tone. You may be able to predict that with no directive or with a private directive (spoken so only the student can hear), the behavior will not occur. Another antecedent for problem behavior may be an assignment that is difficult for the student. When the student is given simple work, she works on it without exhibiting the behavior.

Setting events may happen long before the behavior occurs but may affect the likelihood of its occurrence. Identifying setting events can help identify when a problem behavior may occur. For example, if a student usually displays problem behavior on a certain day of the week, you may find that he stays with a relative in a particularly rowdy household or that the behavior happens when the student is tired or hungry. By identifying these factors, a teacher can address these needs, thereby reducing the likelihood the problem behavior will occur.

Problem Behaviors: This section allows the teacher to identify the behaviors of concern in objective, concrete terms. Attributions such as "stubborn" should be avoided and are not helpful.

Describe what the behaviors look like (e.g., hitting, running, out of seat, etc.)

FBA Hypothesis

Once the interview process is complete, and you have formed some initial ideas about antecedents and setting events and defined the behavior and its consequences, you are ready to form a hypothesis about the behavior. We call this a "summary statement."

A summary statement is simply the description of the pattern of setting events, antecedents, target behaviors, and consequences. It allows us to learn about the function of a given behavior for an individual student and gives us the information necessary to develop a positive behavior intervention plan. Without an hypothesis or "guess" based on direct observation, there is a serious risk for error. Even with an FBA, we could be wrong about the function of the behavior or why the student keeps doing it in spite of our best efforts to change it. The positive behavior plan is an opportunity for us to implement the hypothesis, and we must be prepared to reanalyze it if our intervention doesn't change the behavior quickly.

A real example illustrates this concept. Scott was displaying violent behavior on a daily basis. When asked to do a language arts task, he tore his paper, threw his pencil, used profanity, and sometimes physically attacked the teacher. The FBA hypothesis was that he wanted teacher and peer attention. His behavior plan contained specific instructions on what to do when Scott acted appropriately: He earned "classroom bucks," which could be spent on board games with his peers or one-on-one time with the teacher. The plan also had specific instructions on what to do when he acted inappropriately: Upon refusal to comply with specific redirection requests from his teacher, he was put in an isolated area where the teacher would discuss the problem with him. When Scott continued to be verbally and physically aggressive, he was be sent home for the remainder of the day. This plan was tried for several weeks until his parents refused to have him sent home day in and day out.

A more in-depth FBA was then conducted. While it confirmed that Scott liked receiving attention from his teacher, peers, and parents when he acted out, the second FBA added a new hypothesis: Scott was trying to avoid language arts activities because they were too difficult. Scott was reevaluated and placed in an appropriate instructional group for reading, spelling, and writing. His schedule of reinforcement was increased so that he could earn classroom bucks much more frequently. The teacher role played with him the consequences if he didn't act appropriately: he was given a short, clear directive to either follow directions or go to the time-out room. There would be no processing or any discussion about the problem behavior. He would not be sent home under any circumstance and would make up the time spent in time out during a preferred activity or after school. Scott quickly became more compliant and academically successful.

Keep in mind that simply developing a positive behavior plan based on an FBA doesn't change behavior. The plan must be implemented across the staff. All adults dealing with the target student must be fully aware of how to interact with the student at all times. This in no way threatens the integrity of the student. When a student is placed on a special intervention plan, school personnel often express concern about sharing information and violating a student's privacy or confidentiality. Dr. Barbara Bateman has the following to say about this misconception concerning students with an Individualized Education Plan (IEP):

> Many concerns about violating a student's privacy or confidentiality by sharing necessary information among school personnel are simply misplaced. A legal exception exists specifically to allow this sharing, with or without parental consent. IDEA [Individuals with Disability Education Act] properly requires that IEPs be accessible to all school employees who have a legitimate educational interest in them (Bateman & Golly, 2003, p. 48).

When a positive behavioral intervention plan has been developed for a student who is not on an IEP, it should be shared with all adults who need to know. Consistency in implementing the plan is crucial to its success. Inconsistency can cause the inappropriate behavior to become more severe and more frequent.

Gathering Information

As we mentioned earlier, in order to develop an effective positive behavior plan, getting information from an FBA is essential. The **Information to Develop an Individual Positive Behavior Plan** form at the end of this chapter provides an information-gathering plan. The purpose of this information is to complete a **Summary Statement** form. From the summary statement, the positive behavior plan is developed. (Specific steps and information on how to develop the positive behavior plan will be discussed in Chapter 16.) Figures 21 and 22 show examples of a completed behavior plan and its accompanying summary statement.

Activity

Information Gathering Plan and Summary Statement

- Choose a student with a chronic challenging behavior.

- Gather as much information as possible using the Information to **Develop an Individual Positive Behavior Plan** form (see Figure 21 for an example).

- Reach consensus with others who work with this student.

- Develop a Summary Statement using the **Summary Statement** form (see Figure 22 for a model).

After the best guess has been made about each part of the summary statement, a positive behavior intervention plan can be developed. The next chapter will provide you with the necessary tools.

Figure 21

Information to Develop an
Individual Positive Behavior Plan (Example)

Student Name: _Siefke_   Grade: _4_

Reported by: _Nico Johnson_   Date: _____

1. Description of student:

   - What are the strengths (e.g., academic, artistic, personal)? _Positive, friendly, artistic_

   - What does he/she like to do (e.g., read books, play guitar, draw, do puzzles, ride skateboard, use computer)? _draw, snacks, trinkets_

   - Who does he/she like (e.g., particular peer, principal, staff member)? _____ _Mr. B. 5th grade teacher and Scott Staals_

   - What food/drinks does he/she like? _ice cream, hamburgers, lemon soda_

   - What is home life like? _Dad is in jail, Siefke lives with working mom, no siblings_

2. Present level of functioning:

   - Which academic areas (e.g., reading, math, social studies) are working for him/her? _Below grade level on reading and math but making progress_

   - Which academic areas are difficult for him/her? _receptive and written language_

   - How is he/she being helped in these areas? _Siefke is getting help from the resource room in all academic areas._

   - What kind of social/behavioral problems does he/she have? _Siefke blurts things out impulsively and constantly interrupts the teacher._

3. Describe the problems:

   - What do they look like (e.g., hitting, cussing, running away)? _Talks out_

- Where does he/she have problems (e.g., playground, cafeteria, classroom, locker area, before or after school)? In the classroom.

- Who is usually around when the problem happens (e.g., teacher, assistant, peers)? Classroom teachers

- What time of day does it usually happen? During instructional time

4. What typically happens when he/she gets into trouble? The teacher tells him not to interrupt.

5. How often do these problems take place? Every day

When as much as possible of the above information has been gathered, the following summary can be made:

- **Setting Events:** Things that are going on at home or before the student gets to school that may have an effect later in the day (e.g., home stress, fight with parents/peers, lack of sleep, medication). Dad's in jail

- **Antecedent:** What typically makes the student act inappropriately (e.g., a direction, a task, a person)? Teacher presence during class time

- **Problem Behavior:** What does the student typically do that is inappropriate (e.g., talk back, whine, run away)? He talks out

- **Consequence:** After the incident, what typically happens (e.g., send to office, time out, parent contact, scolding)? Teacher tells him not to interrupt and to raise his hand

- **Maintaining Function:** Why does he/she misbehave (e.g., to get attention, to have power/control, to get out of doing a task)? Siefke wants adult attention

Figure 22

Summary Statement (Example)

Setting Event (What might be happening at home or before school?)	Predictor (What sets student off?)	Problem Behavior (What does student do that is not appropriate?)	Consequence (What happens right after the inappropriate behavior?)	Maintaining Function (What does student want?)
Dad's in jail	Teacher is instructing	Siefke talks out and interrupts the teacher	Teacher tells him to stop	Adult attention

Information to Develop an Individual Positive Behavior Plan

Student Name: _____ Grade: _____

Reported by: _____ Date: _____

1. Description of student:

   • What are the strengths (e.g., academic, artistic, personal)? _____
   _____

   • What does he/she like to do (e.g., read books, play guitar, draw, do puzzles, ride skateboard, use computer)? _____
   _____

   • Who does he/she like (e.g., particular peer, principal, staff member)? _____
   _____

   • What food/drinks does he/she like? _____
   _____

   • What is home life like? _____
   _____

2. Present level of functioning:

   • Which academic areas (e.g., reading, math, social studies) are working for him/her? _____
   _____

   • Which academic areas are difficult for him/her? _____
   _____

   • How is he/she being helped in these areas? _____
   _____

   • What kind of social/behavioral problems does he/she have?_____
   _____

3. Describe the problems:

   • What do they look like (e.g., hitting, cussing, running away)? _____
   _____

- Where does he/she have problems (e.g., playground, cafeteria, classroom, locker area, before or after school)? _____

  _____

- Who is usually around when the problem happens (e.g., teacher, assistant, peers)? _____

  _____

- What time of day does it usually happen? _____

  _____

4. What typically happens when he/she gets into trouble? _____

   _____

5. How often do these problems take place? _____

   _____

When as much as possible of the above information has been gathered, the following summary can be made:

- **Setting Events:** Things that are going on at home or before the student gets to school that may have an effect later in the day (e.g., home stress, fight with parents/peers, lack of sleep, medication). _____

  _____

- **Antecedent:** What typically makes the student act inappropriately (e.g., a direction, a task, a person)?_____

  _____

- **Problem Behavior:** What does the student typically do that is inappropriate (e.g., talk back, whine, run away)?_____

  _____

- **Consequence:** After the incident, what typically happens (e.g., send to office, time out, parent contact, scolding)? _____

  _____

- **Maintaining Function:** Why does he/she misbehave (e.g., to get attention, to have power/control, to get out of doing a task)?_____

  _____

Summary Statement

Setting Event (What might be happening at home or before school?)	Predictor (What sets student off?)	Problem Behavior (What does student do that is not appropriate?)	Consequence (What happens right after the inappropriate behavior?)	Maintaining Function (What does student want?)

chapter 16

Building Positive Behavior Support Plans for Challenging Students

Chapter Objectives:

- ○ Describe the logical link from functional assessment to positive supports

- ○ Describe the components of an effective behavior plan

- ○ Discuss things adults can do to bring about change in student behavior

- ○ Learn to make problem behaviors irrelevant, ineffective, and inefficient by teaching replacement behaviors

Positive behavior support planning is the process of taking the information collected through the FBA process and turning it into a logical plan. As educators, we can alter certain features of the student's environment in order to produce positive behavior change. In the FBA process, these features are referred to as setting events, antecedents, and consequences. You learned about these in the previous section on thinking functionally about behavior. We will explore each of these and discuss ways to

manipulate them in order to produce positive behavior change. In addition, when developing a behavior support plan, we must always consider the resources we have available. Specifically, these are the people and time that can be devoted to teaching the student and arranging the environment.

Figure 23 presents the "big ideas" about behavior supports.

Figure 23

Big Ideas About Positive Behavior Supports

- We need to understand why problem behavior works for the student.

- ICE (Instruction, Curriculum, and Environment) outlines the changes we can make.

- Behavior support should make problem behaviors irrelevant, ineffective, and inefficient.

- Behavior support procedures should always teach a new way to behave.

Considerations When Designing a Behavior Support Plan

As we discussed in Chapter 15, consequences should not be based on what the teacher *thinks* is aversive or rewarding but on what actually changes the behavior. For example, if you keep a student in for recess for a behavior problem and the problem doesn't get better, the student may not mind staying in for recess. If the student is acting out at recess to avoid peers (whining, pushing people away), then recess inside will probably make the behavior worse. Or, if a student is talking out in class for teacher attention and the consequence for this behavior is the teacher talking with the student outside the classroom, once again the behavior will probably persist. You know when you've found an effective consequence when you see a change in behavior. For this reason, keeping a record of the behavior after the plan is in place is essential.

A behavior support plan should make the student's behaviors irrelevant, ineffective, and inefficient (Crone & Horner, 2003; O'Neill et al., 1997). For example, if a student talks out to get attention, teach the student to seek attention more appropriately. By giving the student attention when he raises his hand and not when he calls out, you have made the problem behavior irrelevant and ineffective. If the new behavior works better for your student (he gets attention more quickly), then the behavior has become inefficient. This learning takes time; it is important to reinforce even small changes in behavior.

The acronym **ICE** is a useful reminder that a positive behavior support plan looks at ways to modify the **I**nstruction (how you teach), **C**urriculum (what you teach), and **E**nvironment (where you teach).

The Link Between Behavior Functions and Support Strategies

It is critical to provide a logical link between the function of student behavior and our strategy. As we have shown, if we don't understand why the behavior works for the student, we may choose strategies that actually reward the problem rather than reduce it.

Please take a moment to review Table 3 to understand the link between behavioral function and support strategy. Listed in the table are intervention strategies to address two different behavioral functions. If the function of the behavior is to obtain attention or a tangible reward, the teacher should use the strategies listed to teach students positive alternatives to getting attention or obtaining tangibles. If the function of the behavior is to escape or avoid an instructional demand or undesirable situation, the teacher should use those strategies to decrease the need of the student to escape or avoid the undesirable situation.

Function and Behavior

	Function of Behavior Is to Obtain Attention or Tangible Reward	Function of Behavior Is to Escape/Avoid as a Result of Instructional Demand or Undesirable Situation
Universal Interventions (all students)	• Recognize students for following school behavior expectations • Ignore minor problem behaviors in classrooms and common areas, praise others for correct behavior • Teach students an acceptable alternative to the problem behavior • Provide classwide rewards for following school behavior expectations	• Recognize students for compliance with instructions • Teach students to ask for help rather than acting-out when instruction is too difficult (be responsible) • Adapt instruction so it is less difficult or boring • Recognize or reward students when they are using the desired behavior (be respectful) • Initially remove or reduce demands and then gradually reintroduce them • Provide classwide rewards for working hard, completing tasks, etc.
Selected and Targeted Interventions (some students)	• Teach the student an acceptable alternative to the problem behavior • Briefly deny access to the activity or tangible (time out) • Briefly remove or restrict the student from your/other students' attention (time out) • Provide a school-based adult mentor • Have students "check in" with a behavior card with each teacher during the day • Use an individual-token economy, earning points for acceptable behavior • Teach peers to ignore the problem behavior of the student	• Recognize the student for compliance to instructions • Teach the student to ask for help rather than acting out when instruction is too difficult (be responsible) • Use an individual-token economy, earning points for acceptable behavior (e.g., asking for help) • Adapt instruction so it is less difficult or boring • Provide additional instruction in difficult subjects • Recognize or reward the student for desired behavior (be respectful) • Initially remove or reduce demands and then gradually reintroduce them • Provide classwide or group rewards for working hard, completing tasks, etc. • Interrupt and redirect the student to task • Teach students to self-manage work completion so they don't get behind • Avoid using time out for escape-motivated students

Developing the Plan

Implementing solutions is the process of putting the behavior support plan on paper. Remember that behavior support planning is a continuous process and it is normal to experience glitches with your plan initially.

A good plan will address the following:

- Procedures for increasing desired behavior

- Changes to the ICE (Instruction, Curriculum, Environment)

- Positive consequences for desired behavior

- Procedures for responding to inappropriate behavior

Think about ways to prevent the behavior, how to teach and acknowledge the expected behavior, and how you and others will respond when the problem behavior occurs.

Many behavior support plans fail because they aren't explicit enough about how to implement the intervention and who will be responsible for what. It is necessary to clearly specify who is involved and how their behavior needs to be taught and changed. For example: The problem behavior is talking out and the student has been explicitly taught to raise a hand quietly instead of talking out. If the teacher is not committed to completely ignoring talk outs and reinforcing the student when she is quiet, the plan will fail. The people involved must know exactly what to do, how to do it, and when. They must also agree to make the necessary changes in their behavior. Should the teacher give a reward after the student has an outburst and suddenly becomes quiet? Should the student be rewarded in all classes or just a select few where the problem is the most acute? These are questions that must be answered before the plan gets implemented.

The teacher or the team also need to answer the following questions:

- What are the student's strengths?

- What are the problem behaviors?

- What do we want him/her to do?

- How will we teach the desired behavior?

- What can he/she earn?

- What happens if he/she displays unacceptable behaviors?

- How will the plan be measured?

- How long will the plan be tried?

Figure 24, A Behavior Plan for Siefke, uses the information provided in Chapter 15 to create a behavior plan. An excellent resource for more examples and specific behavior plans is *Why Johnny Doesn't Behave: Twenty Tips and Measurable BIPs* by Barbara Bateman and Annemieke Golly (2003).

Figure 24

A Behavior Plan for Siefke

Student Name: _Siefke_____ Age: _10_ Grade: _4_ Date: _1/11/04_

What are the student's strengths? _Positive, friendly, and artistic_
_____

What are the problem behaviors? _Siefke blurts things out impulsively_
and constantly interrupts the teacher.

What do we want him to do? _Siefke needs to raise his hand in class to_
get permission to talk.

How will we teach the desired behavior? _The teacher will role play with_
Siefke how to raise his hand appropriately. The teacher will demonstrate
the acceptable and unacceptable ways of how and when to raise his
hand for permission to talk.

What can he earn? _Siefke can earn a star each time he raises his hand_
quietly at an appropriate time. When he has earned his goal of 20 stars,
he can spend two minutes talking to the teacher about a subject of his
choice.

What happens if he displays unacceptable behavior? _The teacher will_
not pay attention (planned ignoring) to Siefke when he talks out or
interrupts.

How will the plan be measured? _The teacher will collect data on how_
quickly Siefke reaches his goal of raising his hand 20 times. The teacher
will also collect data on how often he talks out without raising his hand.

How long will the plan be tried? _The teacher will keep track of Siefke's_
talk-outs and when he quietly raises his hand. The plan will be evaluated
in one week.

Data collection: ___The teacher tracks both talk-outs and hand raises.___
___We hope to see the talk-outs decrease and the hand raises increase.___

Siefke's data:

Date	Hand raises	Talk-outs	Comments
Oct 5	*******	/////	
Oct. 6	*******	///	
Oct. 7	*****/*****	//	Earned 2 min. with teacher
Oct 8	***************	/	Earned 2 min. with teacher
Oct. 9	*********/***		No talk-outs all morning. Earned 2 min. with teacher
Oct. 12	********		No talk-outs all day. Earned 10 min. with Mr. B.

Follow-up: ___This is a common problem and a simple plan. The critical ingre-___
___dient is the role playing to teach Siefke how to perform appropriately. After___
___the teacher has demonstrated the skill, Siefke needs to demonstrate the___
___skill several times during role play with lots of positive feedback from the___
___teacher. Too often it is assumed that the child knows how to perform but___
___chooses not to do so.___

___If Siefke's talk-outs decrease significantly, the plan can be allowed to fade___
___out. For example, after five days if he has no talk-outs in the morning, he can___
___earn two minutes talking to his teacher (he loves adult attention). After___
___one week, if he has had no talk-outs all day, he can earn ten minutes with Mr.___
___B. (his favorite teacher) during recess. The teacher must continue to give___
___Siefke opportunities to gain teacher attention appropriately and reinforce___
___him intermittently when he is doing well. For example, once in a while the___
___teacher may say: "Siefke, you are being so respectful by raising your hand___
___when you want my attention, would you like to walk with me when we go out___
___to recess and talk to me for a while?"___

Questions About Your Student With Challenging Behaviors

Think of a student with challenging behaviors and answer the following questions as completely as possible using Figure 24 as a model.

Student Name: _____ Age: ___ Grade: ___ Date: _____

What are the student's strengths? _____

_____

What are the problem behaviors? _____

_____

What do we want him to do? _____

_____

How will we teach the desired behavior? _____

_____

_____

_____

What can he earn?_____

_____

_____

_____

What happens if he displays unacceptable behavior? _____

_____

_____

_____

How will the plan be measured? _____

_____

_____

How long will the plan be tried?_____

_____

_____

Now that you have gathered information on your student, you are ready to assign tasks to the implementation team. The **10-Point Support Plan** form that follows has been helpful and effective when teams use it to execute a positive behavior plan.

10-Point Support Plan

Activity	Person Responsible	Time Line	Completed
1. Clearly define expected behaviors. (What do you want to see, what do you want to hear?)			
2. Teach or role play expected behaviors.			
3. Develop a menu of rewards. (What does student want to work for?)			
4. Develop a point system.			
5. Develop consequences (i.e., bottom line).			
6. Develop flow chart.			
7. Develop data collection system.			
8. Develop time line.			
9. Set next meeting date.			
10. Share plan with parents if possible.			

After implementing the plan according to the time line, evaluate the plan and see if any changes need to be made. Most students who need to increase positive behavior and decrease inappropriate behavior respond well to a clear and concise plan that meets their individual needs.

Charting Individual Students

The sample **Individual Student Plan** that follows can be adapted for individual students. Refer to Figure 25 for a sample point chart for tracking progress.

Individual Student Plan

Behavior goals:

1. Follow Directions.

   • When a teacher asks me to do something, I do it.

2. Be Safe.

   • I walk quietly and safely in classrooms, in hallways, and on breezeways.

3. Be Responsible.

   • I raise my hand and wait for permission to talk.

4. Be Respectful.

   • I keep my hands, feet, objects, and inappropriate comments to myself.

Positive consequences:

I will:

   • Receive positive attention from adults and students.

   • Receive 2 points per period if my behavior is acceptable.

   • Earn the privilege to participate with the rest of the class throughout the day.

   • Earn special activities at school (e.g., computer time or free time).

- Earn special activities at home (e.g., special story, visit from friend, movie, or favorite treat).

Negative consequences:

I will receive:

- Minus 1 point: Warning for behavior change.

- Minus 2 points: If my behavior does not change, privilege to be part of the group is lost, and I must report to the desk in the back of the room.

If my behavior is disruptive, I must go and work in the back of another classroom or other designated quiet place. Teacher or principal will make this decision.

Figure 25

Sample Individual Student Point Chart

Student Name: _Sam Stubborn_   Date: _Jan. 10–Jan 15_

Period	Monday	Tuesday	Wednesday	Thursday	Friday	Total
7:50–8:25 Opening	2	2	2	2	2	10
8:25–9:25 Reading	2	2	2	2	2	10
9:25–10:10 P.E.	0	1	0	0	1	2
10:10–11:00 Computer	2	2	2	2	2	10
11:00–11:20 Language	0	2	2	1	2	7
11:20–11:40 Lunch	2	2	2	2	2	10
11:40–11:55 Recess	2	2	2	2	2	10
11:55–12:15 Social studies	2	2	2	0	1	7
12:15–1:00 Math	0	0	1	0	1	2
1:00–1:55 Science	2	2	2	2	2	10

Note: 0, 1, or 2 points were awarded for accomplishments during each period. Sam can earn 10 maximum points for each period, for a total of 100 points. The agreement made with Sam was as follows: 70–80 points, earn 20 minutes of extra computer time; 80–90 points, earn 30 minutes of extra computer time; 90–100 points, earn lunch with a friend in the classroom. The chart shows that Sam earned 78 points for the week of January 10–15. He earned 20 minutes of extra computer time.

The points on Sam's card show that he is having a more difficult time during P.E. and math. The teacher needs to analyze what might be happening during those periods and make changes to help Sam be more successful during those periods.

Use the blank **Individual Student Point Chart** at the end of this chapter to measure behaviors in your school.

Individual Student Point Chart

Student Name: _____ Date: _____

Period	Monday	Tuesday	Wednesday	Thursday	Friday	Total

chapter 17

Adapting Curricula to Prevent Problem Behavior

Chapter Objectives:

❍ Describe classes of adaptation that can prevent problem behavior

❍ Outline a process for adapting curricula and instruction

❍ Develop and adapt a classroom lesson to prevent problem behavior

One of the principal reasons that students misbehave in school is instruction that is too difficult or poorly adapted. Teachers may think that adapting curricula and instruction is very complicated or time consuming. This does not have to be the case! We have found that effective teachers adapt instruction for all students by using good problem-solving techniques. Good problem solvers can quickly identify the issue, generate alternative solutions, and try one or two to see if they work. In the case of preventing problem behavior, we recommend this process of "try and test" rather than investing a lot of time in complicated, but rarely sustainable, behavioral strategies. Curriculum adaptation can maximize success and participation for

students who are not getting the lesson content or not learning important skills from lessons designed for most students in the class.

Following are some assumptions about curriculum adaptation:

- We have to "meet" the student at his/her current level of performance.

- Poorly adapted instruction is difficult or boring instruction.

- Difficult or boring instruction is aversive.

- Aversive instruction promotes problem behavior:

    —Too much behavior (errors, acting-out)

    —Not enough behavior (inaccurate, poor quality, social withdrawal, or lack of effort)

Cole, Horvath, Chapman, Deschenes, Ebeling, & Sprague (2000) developed a simple problem-solving strategy for quickly developing successful adaptations to curricula and instruction using a matrix of twelve strategies for increasing academic success. We will review the basic strategies and then practice using them. Table 4 provides definitions and examples of curriculum adaptations. Review each one carefully and think about how you would use the strategy to adapt the curriculum for one of your students. Later, you will be asked to practice the strategies.

Table 4

Classes of Curriculum Adaptation

Change the Context	Change the Presentation	Change Behavior Expectations or Consequences
Precorrect Errors Give extra practice for errors you anticipate before instruction. *Before instruction begins, Tamara asks Mitch to sit down and practice "stay in seat" and "keep hands and feet to self" before the lesson starts.*	**Task Difficulty** Adapt the skill level, problem type, or rules to increase accuracy (>75%). *Jeff is allowed to use a calculator to figure math problems to decrease difficulty and his motivation to escape the task. His teacher gradually increases the difficulty and allows him to practice problems without the calculator.*	**Time to Complete** Adapt the time allotted and allowed for learning, task completion, or testing. *Stephen can complete his seatwork with few errors but it takes him longer than other students. His teacher gives him extra time, and he doesn't lose any credit.*
Level of Participation Adapt the extent to which a learner is actively involved in a task or activity. *Pam is very shy about raising her hand in class, so the teacher allows her to write down the answer on a card. She is less anxious and does not act out during lecture.*	**Task Size** Adapt the number of items that a learner is expected to complete or master. *Joe has difficulty completing the entire social studies assignment, so his teacher allows him to complete half to maintain his motivation for learning.*	**Output Method** Adapt how the learner can respond to instruction. *Leslie will often use inappropriate words when asked to speak in front of the class without notes. Her teacher allows her to write her comments and read them instead.*
Alternate Goal Adapt the goals or expectations while using the same materials. *In social studies, Ceci is expected to locate just the states while others locate the capitals as well. When she is successful, she makes fewer bids for peer attention during cooperative group activities.*	**Input Method** Adapt the way instruction is delivered to the learner. *Tom has a hard time tolerating morning circle, often getting up and running away. He is allowed to stay at his desk and learn about the schedule for the class that day.*	**Increase Rewards for Acceptable Behavior** Make doing expected behaviors more valuable than errors or other problem behavior. *Even though Kindle hates to complete math worksheets and often tosses them on the floor, she will complete them if she can earn five extra minutes of recess on Friday.*
Substitute Curricula Provide different instruction and materials. *John is in high school and at risk for dropout. He is introduced to a self-directed curriculum based on computer. He can see his accomplishments clearly and is very motivated to earn high school credits.*	**Level of Support** Increase the amount of personal assistance provided to the learner. *José is given a peer tutor for extra practice in reading grade-level material.*	**Remove or Restrict** Take away desired objects or activities when problem behavior is observed. *George has difficulty with botany facts but can do the work if he is motivated. He and his teacher agree that he will lose five minutes of lunch any day he refuses to complete the daily quiz.*

From Cole, S., Horvath, B., Chapman, C., Deschenes, C., Ebeling, D.G., & Sprague, J. (2000). *Adapting curriculum and instruction in inclusive classrooms: A teacher's desk reference* (2nd ed.). Bloomington, IN: Indiana Institute on Disability and Community. Adapted with permission.

199

Seven Steps for Adapting Curricula and Instruction

Deschenes, Ebeling, & Sprague (1994) outlined seven simple steps for adapting curricula to support inclusion. We have changed these steps to address behavioral support issues. Each of the 12 curriculum adaptation strategies defined in Table 4 can be used in several combinations to make instruction more tolerable and thereby prevent problem behavior. The seven steps for adapting curricula are:

1. Select the subject area.

2. Select the topic.

3. Identify the goal for most learners.

4. Develop the lesson plan for most learners.

5. Identify learners who will need adaptations in curricula or instruction.

6. Choose an appropriate mix of adaptations.

7. Evaluate the effectiveness of the adaptations.

The following curriculum adaptation form, **Adapting Instruction to Minimize Problem Behavior and Maximize Student Success**, includes space to plan the seven steps for adapting curricula and instruction.

Adapting Instruction to Minimize Problem Behavior and Maximize Student Success

1. Select the subject area (and grade level) to be taught:

   ○ Reading ○ Math ○ Science ○ Social Studies ○ Writing

   ○ Music ○ Health ○ P.E. ○ Art ○ Other (specify): _____

   Grade Level: _____

2. How will the lesson be taught (in one day)? _____

   What is the format (e.g., whole class, small group, individual)? _____
   _____

   What will students do?

   ○ Permanent products (e.g., worksheets)

   ○ Listen

   ○ Seatwork

   ○ Cooperative group activity

   ○ Other

3. Describe the instructional plan for most learners. List learner objectives and activities. _____
   _____
   _____
   _____

4. Identify the student who will need adaptations in the curriculum or instructional plan in order to reduce problem behavior and enhance learning and participation.
   Student Name: _____

5. Provide a summary statement regarding the student with problem behavior.

When (the predictor) happens	Student performs (behavior)	In order to get/avoid (attention, the task, etc.)

6. Now use the 12 types of adaptations as a means of thinking about some ways you could adapt what or how you teach to support this learner for this lesson. Try to put one idea in each box. Some strategies may overlap.

Precorrect Errors	Task Difficulty	Time to Complete
Level of Participation	Task Size	Output Method
Alternate Goal	Input Method	Increase Rewards for Acceptable Behavior
Substitute Curriculum	Level of Support	Remove or Restrict

7. **Evaluate your adaptation:** Teachers have found this simple problem-solving process to be quick and effective in reducing mild behavioral problems. The curriculum adaptation strategy can be used prior to implementing the more complex and formal functional assessment process (Chapters 15 and 16). Please take a moment to reflect on the following questions regarding your curriculum or instructional adaptation.

a. Will this adaptation improve the level of participation in class for the student?

b. Is this adaptation the least intrusive (i.e., least interfering) option?

c. Will this adaptation give the student a variety of options, or will the same adaptation be used for all activities (e.g., always do, less problems)?

d. Does the adaptation ensure an appropriate level of difficulty for the student?

e. Can the student use this adaptation in other classes or activities?

chapter 18

Teaching Students Who Are At Risk to Self-Manage Their Behavior

Chapter Objectives:

○ Describe the purposes and benefits of teaching self-management

○ Describe the core features of self-management programs

○ Illustrate how to design and teach a self-management program

Many of us hope that our students will become self-directed, intrinsically motivated learners. Walker (1995) indicates that teachers value compliance to reasonable requests and students who are prepared for class and do their best to complete assigned work. Safe, respectful, and responsible students learn to self-manage their behavior. Students who are good managers of their behavior can also learn to manage their own learning (to the extent you are comfortable).

A Good Method for Recognizing a Student With Behavior Problems

Students who are "off track" may be observed being told:

- What to do.

- How to do it.

- When to do it.

- When not to do it.

- If they did it correctly or not.

Often, when behavioral problems persist, we tend to "tighten the noose" in an effort to control students and get them engaged in the learning process and back on track to compliance. For these students, constant direction from adults may create a situation that promotes "escape" in the form of problem behavior, withdrawal, or lack of motivation. Other students may simply lack the skills of self-management and need to be taught. If we are to help our students achieve self-control and intrinsic motivation, we will need to teach students with problem behavior to respond more independently and to manage their own behavior and school work. We should not assume that they know how to do this or that they purposely are not managing their own behavior.

What Is Self-Management?

A student who is a good self-manager is able to (with a little help from the teacher) identify problems to be solved (e.g., not getting work done, not prepared for class), identify alternative behaviors (e.g., work without interruption for 15 minutes, use a checklist to assure that all materials are ready for class), and arrange contingencies to change those behaviors (e.g., enjoy the "reward" of a job well done, gain access to the computer, or free time after work completion).

Why Teach Self-Management and Self-Control?

Teaching self-management has multiple practical benefits in the classroom. It is an effective curriculum adaptation for many problems and is a way to make "thinking" overt, so you can teach the student to "think aloud" or on paper at first, and then fade to independent performance. Self-management is an excellent way to replace adult-mediated behavior, thus minimizing teacher–student conflicts over control of a situation or task. Self-management also promotes independence now and in the future, and teaches positive social behavior. Finally, self-management routines can minimize interactions during classroom routines, reducing noise and distraction in the classroom.

Self-Management Components

There are four major self-management components:

1. Self-monitoring

2. Self-recording

3. Self-evaluation

4. Self-delivery of reinforcement

Each is defined with an example in the following sections.

Self-Monitoring (What do I do?/What am I doing?)

Self-monitoring is the first step in self-management. The student learns to discriminate between correct and incorrect performance of skills or behaviors. For example, a student may count the number of problems completed on a math worksheet, or the number of times he/she talks out in class without being recognized. Self-monitoring may be occasioned by external (cues, checklists) or internal (thoughts) events.

This may sound simplistic, but many students may not be aware of their own behavior and need to learn to observe when they are performing acceptable or unacceptable behavior. For example, students who talk out of turn in class often may not be aware of the frequency or volume of their talk outs, and may also not understand the impact of the behavior. We generally recommend that an external cue or checklist be used initially to simplify monitoring and compliance to the routine.

Self-Recording

In self-recording, the student notes what she is doing. The most common method is some type of paper-and-pencil checklist, although a device such as a golf counter or even a computer sound can be used. For many of us, the date book or task list is a great example of a self-recording device. It is commonly demonstrated in research that taking data on oneself has reactive effects; that is, once you start paying attention to a behavior and counting or recording it, you may do less of the behavior for a while. This reactivity usually wears off unless there is some form of prompting or a source of reward for continuing to count (e.g., "I get better and stay better."). For example, an adult attempting to quit smoking may count the number of cigarettes smoked in a day in an effort to use less tobacco. For a few days, this might work, but without some motivation, the effect will be short lived. In the classroom, we may ask a student to count talk outs, but this habit will soon fade unless all of the self-management components are put into place. Now, take a moment to complete the following reflection.

Reflection

Self-Management

1. What are ways that you self-record in your life?

2. How do you keep track of your daily tasks or long-term projects?

3. How do you promote self-management in your classroom now?

Setting up self-recording. The following steps illustrate the process for setting up self-recording:

1. Identify a specific behavior (e.g., talking out in class).

2. Detect whether the behavior has occurred (provide the student with a definition of talking out, and demonstrate examples and nonexamples).

3. Make a record of the behavior.

   • Mark a card or chart upon behavior completion.

   • Use a counter device.

Self-Evaluation (How did I do?)

In the self-evaluation step, the student evaluates his behavior in relation to a criterion, determining if behavior is correct or appropriate according to the criteria you have set. This is the toughest step!

Using the "talking out" example above: If the student does or does not talk out in class, at the end of an interval (two minutes, for example), the student must judge whether the behavior occurred or not and evaluate his/her performance. This judgment provides the basis for self-recording and later self-delivery of reward. You will need to review self-evaluation frequently with the student. But be aware that the most important step in teaching self-evaluation is to let the student self-evaluate before you give any feedback.

Self-Delivery of Reinforcement (What happens when I do it?)

The most satisfying step in self management is to deliver a reward or recognition to yourself! Self-delivered consequences are the same as any others and may include tangible/material rewards, self-praise, moving on to the next step or activity, or simply checking off a job well done. One way to determine if simply checking off a task is a reward is to ask others if they ever have put a task on their list and checked it off after it was already done. Other examples are listed below:

   • Student self-delivers coins or tokens upon completion of tasks or items.

   • Student analyzes performance records (e.g., homework completed, fewer talk outs) and takes some free time (under agreement with the teacher).

   • Student delivers a praise statement to himself/herself.

207

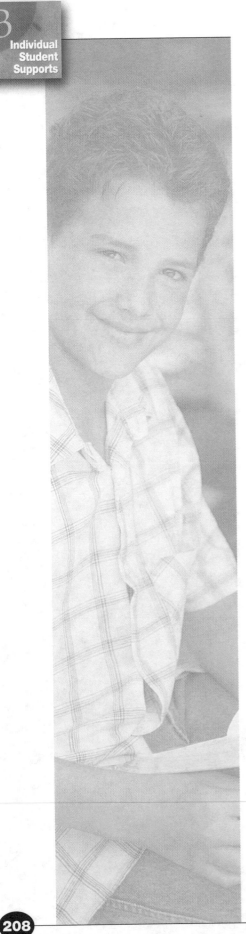

- Student asks for feedback from the teacher by raising hand (teacher knows to come over and recognize the accomplishment).

Setting Up and Building a Self-Management Routine

Now that you have the basics, you can begin building self-management systems for your students. The big steps are:

- Select a behavior that needs changing (you can decide yourself or negotiate with the student).

- Select an alternative behavior that either replaces or competes with the behavior that needs changing. For example, raising a hand is a replacement for talking out; staying in seat competes with getting out of seat.

- Teach the student to self-monitor (become aware of) the behavior. Use the same teaching plan you learned in Chapter 6: Teaching Schoolwide Behavior Expectations (e.g., give a rationale, show examples and nonexamples, practice using role play).

- Set a method for recording the behavior(s) and teach the student how to use it (same also as Chapter 6 procedures).

- Coach the student in self-monitoring and recording initially. If you see the student engaging in the target behavior, wait briefly and then remind her to record the event. If the student records independently and correctly, recognize the student.

- Set a criterion for reward and teach the student to track progress. For example, staying in seat nine of ten intervals during seatwork would meet the criterion for five minutes of extra recess.

- You can decide if you want your student to self-deliver a reward or just ask for it when the criteria are met. The sample self-management forms include a place for parent signature. This is a great way to incorporate a delayed reward at home for the child.

The following **Self-Management Checklist 1–4** are samples that you can adapt for use in your classroom. Take a look at how they are set up and then use the development steps outlined in this chapter to build a system for one of your students.

Self-Management Checklist 1

Student Name: _____   Date: _____

Behavior Goals:

1. Arrive on time

2. Complete work

3. Stop and listen

Allow student to rate his/her behavior first. Then initial if you agree.

	Arrive on Time	Complete Work	Stop and Listen	Teacher Initial
Morning Check In	Yes / No	Yes / No	Yes / No	
Math	Yes / No	Yes / No	Yes / No	
Reading	Yes / No	Yes / No	Yes / No	
Social Studies	Yes / No	Yes / No	Yes / No	
Lunch	Yes / No	n/a	Yes / No	
Language Arts	Yes / No	Yes / No	Yes / No	
Music	Yes / No	Yes / No	Yes / No	
Science	Yes / No	Yes / No	Yes / No	
Afternoon Check Out	Yes / No	Yes / No	Yes / No	
Total for Goal	/9	/8	/9	/9

Reward:

_____   _____
Parent Signature   Date

Self-Management Checklist 2

Student Name: _____ Date: _____

Behavior Goals:

Follow directions in class

Allow student to rate his/her behavior first. Then initial if you agree.

	Stop and Listen	Repeat Direction	Ask for Help	Start Right Away	Finish on Time	Teacher Initial
Morning Check In	Yes / No	Yes / No	Yes / No	Yes / No	Yes / No	
Math	Yes / No	Yes / No	Yes / No	Yes / No	Yes / No	
Reading	Yes / No	Yes / No	Yes / No	Yes / No	Yes / No	
Social Studies	Yes / No	Yes / No	Yes / No	Yes / No	Yes / No	
Lunch	Yes / No	Yes / No	Yes / No	Yes / No	Yes / No	
Language Arts	Yes / No	Yes / No	Yes / No	Yes / No	Yes / No	
Music	Yes / No	Yes / No	Yes / No	Yes / No	Yes / No	
Science	Yes / No	Yes / No	Yes / No	Yes / No	Yes / No	
Afternoon Check Out	Yes / No	Yes / No	Yes / No	Yes / No	Yes / No	
Total for Goal	/9	/9	/9	/9	/9	/9

Reward:

_____
Parent Signature   Date

Self-Management Checklist 3

Student Name: _____ Date: _____

Behavior Goals:

Solve problems without getting angry

Allow student to rate his/her behavior first. Then initial if you agree.

Define Problem			Teacher Initial
State "what I need"	Yes / No	Yes / No	
Generate alternative solutions	Yes / No	Yes / No	
Choose a solution	Yes / No	Yes / No	
Evaluate the choice How do I feel? How do others feel?	Yes / No	Yes / No	
Did it work?	Yes / No	Yes / No	
Total for Goal	/5	/5	/5

Reward:

_____

Parent Signature   Date

Self-Management Checklist 4

Student Name: _____ Date: _____

Behavior Goals:

Finish five math problems, and then raise hand.

Allow student to rate his/her behavior first. Then initial if you agree.

Problem 1	Problem 2	Problem 3	Problem 4	Problem 5	Teacher Initial

Reward:

_____

Parent Signature   Date

Schoolwide 1

Classroom Management 2

Individual Student Supports 3

4 Family Support

Family Support

Chapter 19   School/Home Collaboration

chapter 19

School/Home Collaboration

Chapter Objective:

○ Learn procedures to communicate with parents and caregivers about schoolwide discipline

○ Learn do's and don't's of communicating with children

As teachers and educators, we are frequently asked the question: "What is the most frustrating aspect of your job?" The answer is often: "Dealing with parents." But parents are not some creatures from another planet who don't want to cooperate with us. Many teachers are parents themselves. We must try to stand in the shoes of parents when working with students. We must remember that parents know their children better than anyone and are with them many more hours a week than the teacher. Parents are the most important teachers of the child. On the other hand, teachers are experts at knowing and teaching curricula. We need to remember that the main goal of parents and teachers is to help the child be as successful as possible academically and socially. The information in this chapter can be used as a resource when working with parents. Many of the practices may also be helpful for other adults working with children.

The following section provides teachers with tips and effective strategies to work positively

and cooperatively with parents. The goals for this section are to:

- Establish and communicate clear expectations.

- Encourage effective communication between home and school.

- Know what to avoid when dealing with parents.

- Learn the do's and don't's of working with parents.

The common goal of parents/caregivers and teachers is to help children be as successful as possible. Having parents as cooperative partners is very beneficial to a child's progress. The information provided here can be shared with all the significant adults in a student's life. Many children spend a majority of their waking hours in the presence of adults other than their parents. Daycare providers, babysitters, grandparents, aunts, uncles, neighbors, or older siblings may be primary caregivers. In this chapter, we will refer to all caregivers as "parents" and all school staff as "teachers."

Communication Strategies for Teachers

A lack of effective communication too often causes a lack of cooperation between parents and teachers. Providing parents with a copy of school and classroom expectations, routines, and schedules, and requesting a signed verification after reading them, is the first step to effective communication. Inviting parents into the classroom, making positive phone calls, and sending e-mail messages and notes before problems occur establishes positive communication.

Parents often only learn from their child's report what is going on at school. If parents can hear or see firsthand how your classroom is organized, how you have taught expectations, how you interact with all students, and how much work and effort you put into making the classroom a positive and predictable environment, they will understand their child's reports more clearly. Some parents have had negative school experiences themselves or may view teachers as intimidating or have been contacted by the school only when there was a problem. When parents do need to get involved because of a problem, it is much easier if good communication has already been established. Inviting parents to school assemblies and activities when students perform is another way to encourage parents to become involved in a positive way.

In establishing parent cooperation and communication, the teacher needs to:

- Establish positive contact as early as possible (e.g., send home a positive note or e-mail at the beginning of the school year, such as, "John had great ideas during science class.").

- Send home clearly defined school and classroom expectations, routines, and schedules.

- Request verification of your communications.

- Establish an "open door" policy for visits to your classroom. Invite parents to come and visit the classroom anytime.

- Routinely send home positive notes about your students (e.g., "Lucy asked great questions in English class today.").

- Inform parents of small accomplishments (e.g., bringing notebooks to class consistently, asking for help appropriately, helping peers).

- Make positive comments on student papers and assignments (e.g., "You wrote topic sentences with at least three supporting sentences, Carmen. Good for you!").

- Provide opportunities for students to call home to report a positive occurrence.

- Keep data to show parents the positive changes in student behavior and academics. Well-organized graphs speak louder than words.

- Keep things light.

You, as teacher, should also try not to:
- Blame parents for the child's behavior.
- Be authoritarian and give the impression that you know it all.
- React when you don't know all the facts.
- Assume that parents don't want to take responsibility.
- Get into power struggles.

Best Behavior • chapter nineteen

DO	DON'T
View parents as allies.	View parents as enemies.
Communicate clearly and frequently.	Assume what parents "should" know.
Let parents know when the child is doing well.	Call only when there is a problem.
	Assume that parents "don't care."
Realize that some parents have had negative school experiences.	Assume that your concern is the only thing parents are dealing with.
Empathize with parents.	Assume that you have all the answers.
Listen to parents.	
Use humor.	Make mountains out of molehills.
Remember how you want to be treated as a parent.	Treat parents as if they are from another planet.

When dealing with students who display challenging behaviors, remember that parents have had to deal with their child many hours a day for many years. Teachers often blame parents for unacceptable student behavior, while parents often blame teachers for not giving their child needed help. Yet, both parties want the best for the child. Parents, even ineffective ones, want their child to be successful at school. Many children have wonderfully supportive parents who value the importance of being respectful, responsible, and safe in school. The tips provided above will help establish cooperation with many parents. Unfortunately, many students have unsupportive, chaotic home environments, and school is a "safe haven" for them. In spite of our best efforts to communicate with all parents, some will not be reached.

Remember, however, that you must never punish children for having ineffective parents. Teachers are often the only consistent and respectful adult in a child's life. By being clear, consistent, and respectful, teachers can make a huge difference in the lives of even the most disadvantaged students. The following reproducibles may help in your discussions with parents about how they can work with their children at home to develop and strengthen the skills of communication, cooperation, limit setting, problem solving, and confidence building.

Communication

When your child communicates information about what has been going on at school, it gives you a chance to share in your child's successes and help with any problems. Children provide information in many ways: talking, drawing, showing, and even teaching. Parents must teach their children to share from the very first day of preschool and make it a daily practice. Parents need to teach and use specific communication skills to have more in-depth sharing sessions. If these daily sessions are routinely done in a comfortable place at the same time, they will continue throughout the child's entire school career. The following suggestions may help:

DO	DON'T
Offer undivided attention.	Talk about school when you're upset.
Have a quiet place.	Ask your child about school when you're busy.
Make eye contact.	Interrupt your child when he or she is talking to you.
Get comfortable.	
Ask specific questions.	Correct how your child shares information or does the activities.

Cooperation

Cooperation helps children avoid problems. Children who cooperate tend to be more successful and happy in school and in the world. Encouraging cooperation in your child doesn't mean stifling individuality. On the contrary, children who cooperate are better able to adapt and express themselves appropriately. The following suggestions will make it easier for your child to cooperate with your requests:

DO	DON'T
Be close to your child.	Be in another room.
Make eye contact.	Yell.
Use a neutral tone.	Phrase a request as a question.
Make one request at a time.	Ask too many things at once.
Be specific.	Be vague.
Provide positive feedback. Use words like: "I noticed..., I see...."	Use sarcasm.
Catch your child doing the "right" thing.	Make a mountain out of a molehill.

Limit Setting

When expectations, such as getting up and going to bed, eating routines, chores and homework, the use of appropriate language, visiting friends, telephone privileges, are clearly explained, taught, and reinforced, it's easier for children to make choices about their behavior. Parental limits keep children safe and healthy until they achieve independence and the ability to keep themselves safe and healthy. The more clear and consistent your expectations are, the safer the child will feel. If an 8 o'clock bedtime or one hour of TV watching has been established and becomes routine, the child doesn't have to negotiate and argue about bedtime or TV watching. Parents need to continually let their child know when rules are followed and state clear consequences when rules are violated. Negative consequences may include removing privileges (e.g., telephone, TV watching, visiting friends), time-out (e.g., time in a quiet room, loss of time with friends or car), or restitution (e.g., yard work, house cleaning, loss of allowance). When you impose negative consequences, you should do so in a calm, neutral voice without yelling or using harsh words or lecturing. Even if the child begins to resist your request, keep your tone even. It will help to keep you in control of your emotions and will also be an example of self-control for your child. The following suggestions should help you set limits effectively:

DO	DON'T
Use a neutral tone.	Yell.
Use consequences.	Make empty threats.
Provide encouragement.	Call your child names.
Be consistent.	Change your rules when you feel like it.
Know where your child is.	Allow your child to go places that you have no information about.
Know who your child is with.	Allow your child to go to someone's house if you haven't checked with the adults in charge.

Problem Solving

A problem is the difference between what is observed and what is expected. If parents incorporate problem-solving strategies from very early on, children will be able to use these skills and improve on them for the rest of their lives. Parents can help children find a place to start working on a problem so that they can see the possibility of a solution. For example, when Nico is having a hard time building a tower with blocks, his dad helps him start by making the base stronger. This gives Nico a plan to begin. Saying, "Haven't you figured out how to put that together yet?" or "What's wrong? Can't you figure that out? It's so easy," doesn't offer Nico a starting place. The following suggestions should help you help your child problem solve effectively:

DO	DON'T
Target the situation, not the person.	Label the person.
State the problem in a neutral way.	Blame others.
Look for a win/win situation.	Always want to be "right."
Guide your child.	Give all the solutions.
Break the problem into manageable parts.	Attack the whole thing all at once.
	Criticize your child.
Prompt your child. Ask questions that lead to solving problems.	

Confidence Building

Regardless of whether or not you live with your child, it's important that you maintain a positive relationship with the child. A positive relationship gives your child a stable environment in which to grow, so that you are one of the people your child can depend on. The time to begin building on a positive relationship and your child's self-confidence cannot start too early. Parents' messages build children's beliefs about who they are and what they can do in life. When children are experiencing problems getting along, they are usually receiving a lot of negative messages from others. They don't feel good about themselves. Parents can help by pointing out their children's good ideas, positive attributes, and appropriate behaviors. Daily attention for appropriate behavior can help children through difficult times at school and with friends. It is harder to be positive with children who are going through a tough period. Also, it is more difficult to provide positive feedback and compliments to discouraged children. It may take time to figure out ways of encouraging children that are comfortable for both you and your children. The following suggestions can help you build your child's confidence:

DO	DON'T
Look for daily positive behavior.	Compare your child with another child.
Offer opportunities to try new skills.	Use sarcasm with positive feedback.
Make time for your child.	Take over your child's activities.
Ask for your child's ideas and help.	Criticize.

Conclusion

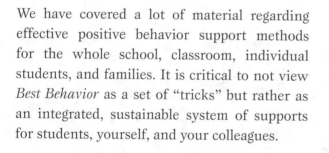

Planning to Sustain and Improve Your Success

Conclusion Objectives:

❍ Review overall goals and content of *Best Behavior*

❍ Review personal and system goals for your next steps in the journey to *Best Behavior* in your school

We have covered a lot of material regarding effective positive behavior support methods for the whole school, classroom, individual students, and families. It is critical to not view *Best Behavior* as a set of "tricks" but rather as an integrated, sustainable system of supports for students, yourself, and your colleagues.

Take some time to reflect on how you might use your new skills and knowledge when you get back to your school. For change to be effective, you need to be able to embed training and support for your colleagues across the school year. When training or coaching your peers, be sure to include theory, modeling, and practice as we have shown you here. Finally, you should allow for team-based planning for implementation.

As your team progresses, members can take on the role of trainers and provide technical assistance on new methods, coteach expected behavior lessons, or observe or coach colleagues. Also consider approving release time for observing or coaching, staff meeting time for discussion and planning, and provision of follow-up training (see Chapter 2 for additional information). Additional support needs for your school may include evaluation, "expert" training and consultation, and family liaison.

Finally, we suggest you return to the **Best Behavior** **Self-Assessment Survey** that you completed in Chapter 4. Review the goals you developed and the action steps you set out there. Take a few minutes to review and modify or change these steps as appropriate. This plan will help you to strategically plan and implement your program.

Bibliography

American Psychological Association. (1993). *Violence and youth: Psychology's response*. Washington, DC: American Psychological Association.

Bateman, B., & Golly, A. (2003). *Why Johnny doesn't behave: Twenty tips for measurable BIPs*. Verona, WI: Attainment Company.

Biglan, A. (1995). Translating what we know about the context of antisocial behavior into a lower prevalence of such behavior. *Journal of Applied Behavior Analysis, 28*, 479–492.

Biglan, A., Metzler, C. W., Rusby, J. C., & Sprague, J. R. (in press). *Evaluation of a comprehensive behavior management program to improve school-wide positive behavior support*. Eugene, OR: Oregon Research Institute and University of Oregon.

Botvan, G. J. (1979). *Life skills training: Promoting health and personal development.* Princeton, NJ: Princeton Health Press, Inc.

Brophy, J., & Good, T. (1996). Teacher behavior and student achievement. In M. C. Wittrock (Ed.), *Handbook of research on training* (pp. 328–375). New York: Macmillan.

Brophy, J., & Good, T. (2000). *Looking in classrooms* (8th ed.). New York: Longman.

Carnine, D., Silbert, J., & Kameenui, E. J. (1997). *Direct instruction reading* (3rd ed.). Upper Saddle River, NJ: Merrill.

Cole, S., Horvath, B., Chapman, C., Deschenes, C., Ebeling, D. G., & Sprague, J. (2000). *Adapting curriculum and instruction in inclusive classrooms: A teacher's desk reference* (2nd ed.). Bloomington, IN: Institute for the Study of Developmental Disabilities.

Colvin, G., (1999). *Defusing anger and aggression: Safe strategies for secondary school educators.* Video. Eugene, OR: IRIS Media.

Colvin, G., (2002). *Defusing anger and aggression: Safe strategies for secondary school educators.* Video. Eugene, OR: IRIS Media.

Colvin, G. (2004). *Managing the cycle of acting-out behavior.* Eugene, OR: Behavior Associates.

Colvin, G., Kameenui, E. J., & Sugai, G. (1993). School-wide and classroom management: Reconceptualizing the integration and management of students with behavior problems in general education. *Education and Treatment of Children, 16,* 361–381.

Colvin, G., & Lazar, M. (1997). *Effective elementary classroom: Managing for success.* Longmont, CO: Sopris West Educational Services.

Colvin, G., Sugai, G., Good, R. H., III, & Lee, Y. (1997). Using active supervision and precorrection to improve transition behaviors in an elementary school. *School Psychology Quarterly, 12,* 344–363.

Committee for Children. (1996). Prevention update. *Newsletter of the Committee for Children, January.* Seattle, WA: Committee for Children.

Committee for Children. (1997). *Second step: Violence prevention curriculum.* Seattle, WA: Committee for Children.

Crone, D. A., & Horner, R. H. (2003). *Building positive behavior support systems in schools: Functional behavioral assessment.* New York: Guilford Press.

Deschenes, C., Ebeling, D., & Sprague, J. (1994). *Adapting curriculum and instruction in inclusive classrooms: A teacher's desk reference.* Bloomington, IN: Institute for the Study of Developmental Disabilities.

Dwyer, K., Osher, D., & Wagner, C. (1998). *Early warning, timely response: A guide to safe schools.* Washington, DC: U.S. Department of Education.

Embry, D. E., Flannery, D., Vazsonyi, A., Powell, K., & Atha, H. (1996). PeaceBuilders: A theoretically driven, school-based model for early violence prevention. *American Journal of Preventive Medicine, 12,* 91–100.

Emmer, E. T., Evertson, C. M., Sanford, J. P., Clements, B. S., & Worsham, M. E. (1984). *Classroom management for secondary teachers.* Englewood Cliffs, NJ: Prentice-Hall.

Evertson, C. M. (1994). Classroom rules and routines. *International Encyclopedia of Education* (2nd ed.). Oxford: Pergamon Press.

Evertson, C. M., Emmer, E. T., Clements, B. S., Sanford, J. P., & Worsham, M. E. (1984). *Classroom management for elementary teachers.* Englewood Cliffs, NJ: Prentice-Hall.

Gottfredson, D. C. (1997). School-based crime prevention. In L. Sherman, D. Gottfredson, D. Mackenzie, J. Eck, P. Reuter, & S. Bushway (Eds.), *Preventing crime: What works, what doesn't, what's promising* (Chap. 5, pp. 1–74). College Park, MD: Department of Criminology and Criminal Justice.

Greenberg, M. T., Domitrovich, C., & Bumbarger, B. (1999). *Preventing mental disorders in school-age children: A review of the effectiveness of prevention programs.* (Report submitted to Center for Mental Health Services, Substance Abuse Mental Health Services Administration). Washington, DC: U.S. Department of Health and Human Services.

Greenwood, C. R., Hops, H., Delquadri, J., & Guild, J. J., (1974). Group contingencies for group consequences in classroom management: A further analysis. *Journal of Applied Behavior Analysis, 7,* 413–425.

Grossman, D. C., Neckerman, H. J., Joepsell, T. D., Liu, P., Asher, K. N., Beland, K., Frey, K., & Rivara, F. P. (1997). Effectiveness of a violence prevention curriculum among children in elementary school. *Journal of the American Medical Association, 277*(20), 1605–1611.

Hagan, S. L. (1998). *An examination of classroom management procedures that support middle school students with severe and chronic problem behaviors.* Eugene, OR: Department of Special Education and Community Resources and the Graduate School, University of Oregon.

Hofmeister, A., & Lubke, M. (1990). *Research into practice: Implementing effective teaching strategies.* Boston: Allyn and Bacon.

Horner, R. H., & Sugai, G. (2000). School-wide behavior support: An emerging initiative (special issue). *Journal of Positive Behavioral Interventions, 2,* 231–233.

Horner, R. H., Sugai, G., & Horner, H. F. (2000). A school wide approach to student discipline. *The School Administrator, 57*(2), 20–24.

Horner, R. H., Sugai, G., & Horner, H. F. (in press). *Administrative leadership can reduce violence in schools.*

Irvin, L. K., Tobin, T. J., Sprague, J. R., & Vincent, C. G. (in press). *Validity of office discipline referrals measures as indices of school-wide behavioral status and effects of school-wide behavioral interventions.* Eugene, OR: University of Oregon OSEP Center on Positive Behavioral Interventions and Supports.

Kellam, S. G., Mayer, L. S., Rebok, G. W., & Hawkins, W. E. (1998). Effects of improving achievement on aggressive behavior and of improving aggressive behavior on achievement through two preventive interventions: An investigation of causal paths. In B. P. Dohrenwend (Ed.), *Adversity, stress, and psychopathology* (pp. 486–505). New York: Oxford University Press.

Langland, S., Lewis-Palmer, T., & Sugai, G. (1998). Teaching respect in the classroom: An instructional approach. *Journal of Behavioral Education, 8,* 245–262.

Latham, G. I. (1992). *Managing the classroom environment to facilitate effective instruction.* Logan, UT: P&T Ink.

Lewis, T. J., Colvin, G. & Sugai, G. (2000). The effects of precorrection and active supervision on the recess behavior of elementary school students. *Education and Treatment of Children, 23,* 109–121.

Lewis, T. J., Sugai, G., & Colvin, G. (1998). Reducing problem behavior through a school-wide system of effective behavioral support: Investigation of a school-wide social skills training program and contextual interventions. *School Psychology Review, 27,* 446–459.

Lewis-Palmer, T., Sugai, G., & Larson, S. (1999). Using data to guide decisions about program implementation and effectiveness. *Effective School Practices, 17*(4), 47–53.

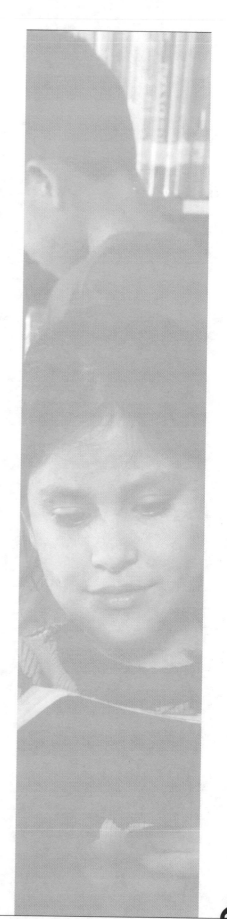

Loeber, R., & Farrington, D. P. (Eds.). (1998). *Serious and violent juvenile offenders: Risk factors and successful interventions*. Thousand Oaks, CA: Sage Publications.

Maag, J. W. (2001). Rewarded by punishment: Reflections on the disuse of positive reinforcement in schools. *Exceptional Children. 67*(2), 173–186.

Madsen, C. H., Becker, W. C., Thomas, D., Koser, L., & Plager, E., (1968). An analysis of the reinforcing function of "sit down" commands. In R. K. Parker (Ed.), *Readings in educational psychology* (pp. 265–278). Boston: Allyn & Bacon.

Mayer, G. R. (1995). Preventing antisocial behavior in the schools. *Journal of Applied Behavior Analysis, 28*(4), 467–478.

Mayer, G. R., Butterworth, T., Nafpaktitis, M., & Sulzer-Azaroff, B. (1983). Preventing school vandalism and improving discipline: A three-year study. *Journal of Applied Behavior Analysis, 16*, 355–369.

Mayer, G. R., & Sulzer-Azaroff, B. (1990). Interventions for vandalism. In G. Stoner, M. R. Shinn, & H. M. Walker (Eds.), *Interventions for achievement and behavior problems* [monograph]. Washington, DC: National Association of School Psychologists.

Mehas, K., Boling, K., Sobieniak, S., Sprague, J., Burke, M. D., & Hagan, S. (1998). Finding a safe haven in middle school: Discipline behavior intervention. *The Council for Exceptional Children, 30*(4), 20–23.

Metzler, C. W., Biglan, A., Rusby, J. C., & Sprague, J. R. (2001). Evaluation of a comprehensive behavior management program to improve school-wide positive behavior support. *Education and Treatment of Children, 24*(4), 448–479.

Morgan, D. P., & Jenson, W. R. (1988). *Teaching behaviorally disordered students: Preferred practices*. Columbus, OH: Merrill Publishing.

National School Safety Center. (1996). *National School Safety Center Newsletter, March*. Malibu, CA: National School Safety Center.

O'Donnell, J., Hawkins, J., Catalano, R., Abbott, R., & Day, L. (1995). Preventing school failure, drug use, and delinquency among low-income children: Long-term intervention in elementary schools. *American Journal of Orthopsychiatry, 65,* 87–100.

Office of Juvenile Justice and Delinquency Prevention. (1995). *Guide for implementing a comprehensive strategy for serious, violent and chronic juvenile offenders.* Washington, DC: Office of Juvenile Justice and Delinquency Prevention.

O'Leary, K. D., Becker, W. C., Evans, M. B., & Saudargas, R. A. (1969). A token reinforcement program in a public school: A replication and systematic analysis. *Journal of Applied Behavior Analysis, 2,* 3–13.

O'Neill, R. E., Horner, R. H., Albin, R. W., Sprague, J. R., Newton, S., & Storey, K. (1997). *Functional assessment and program development for problem behavior: A practical handbook* (2nd ed.). Pacific Grove, CA: Brookes/Cole Publishing.

Patterson, G. R., Reid, J. B., & Dishion, T. J. (1992). *Antisocial boys.* Eugene, OR: Castalia Press.

Rhode, G., Jenson, W. R., & Reavis, H. K. (1992). *The tough kid book: Practical classroom management strategies.* Longmont, CO: Sopris West Educational Services.

Schneider, T., Walker, H. M., & Sprague, J. R. (2000). *Safe school design: A handbook for educational leaders.* Eugene, OR: ERIC Clearinghouse on Educational Management, College of Education, University of Oregon.

Skiba, R. J., Peterson, R. L., & Williams, T. (1997). Office referrals and suspensions: Disciplinary intervention in middle schools. *Education and Treatment of Children, 20,* 295–315.

Sprague, J., Golly, A., Bernstein, L., Munrkes, A. M., & March, R. M. (1999). *Effective school and classroom discipline: A training manual.* Eugene, OR: University of Oregon, Institute on Violence and Destructive Behavior.

Sprague, J. & Smith, S. (2003). *Best Behavior school discipline self-assessment survey*. Eugene, OR: University of Oregon, Institute on Violence and Destructive Behavior.

Sprague, J. R., Sugai, G., Horner, R. H., & Walker, H. M. (1999). Using office discipline referral data to evaluate school-wide discipline and violence prevention interventions. *Oregon School Study Council Bulletin, 42*(2). Eugene, OR: University of Oregon, College of Education.

Sprague, J. R., Sugai, G., & Walker, H. (1998). Antisocial behavior in schools. In T. S. Watson & F. M. Gresham (Eds.), *Handbook of child behavior therapy* (pp. 451–474). New York: Plenum.

Sprague, J., & Walker, H. (2000). Early identification and intervention for youth with antisocial and violent behavior. *Exceptional Children, 66*(3), 367–379.

Sprague, J., Walker, H., Golly, A., White, K., Myers, D., Shannon, T. (2001). Translating research into effective practice: The effects of a universal staff and student intervention on indicators of discipline and school safety. *Education and Treatment of Children, 24*(4), 495–511.

Sprick, R. (1985). *Discipline in the secondary classroom: A problem-by-problem survival guide.* Englewood Cliffs, NJ: Prentice-Hall.

Sprick, R., Garrison, M., & Howard, L. (1998). *CHAMPS: A proactive and positive approach to classroom management.* Longmont, CO: Sopris West Educational Services.

Sprick, R., Garrison, M., & Howard, L. (2000). *ParaPro: Supporting the instructional process.* Longmont, CO: Sopris West Educational Services.

Sprick, R. S., & Howard, L. M. (1995). *The teacher's encyclopedia of behavior management: 100 problems/ 500 plans.* Longmont, CO: Sopris West Educational Services.

Sprick, R., Howard, L., Wise, B. J., Marcum, K., & Haykin, M. (1998). *Administrator's desk reference of behavior management*. Longmont, CO: Sopris West Educational Services.

Sprick, R., Sprick, M., & Garrison, M. (1992a). *Foundations: Developing positive school-wide discipline policies*. Longmont, CO: Sopris West Educational Services.

Sprick, R., Sprick, M., & Garrison, M. (1992b). *Interventions: Collaborative planning for students at risk*. Longmont, CO: Sopris West Educational Services.

Stage, S. A., & Quiroz, D. R. (1997). A meta-analysis of interventions to decrease disruptive classroom behavior in public education settings. *School Psychology Review, 26*(3), 333–368

Sugai, G., & Horner, R. (1994). Including students with severe behavior problems in general education settings: Assumptions, challenges, and solutions. *Oregon Conference Monograph, 6*, 102–120.

Sugai, G., Horner, R. H., Dunlap, G., Hieneman, M., Lewis, T. J., Nelson, C. M., Scott, T., Liaupsin, C., Sailor, W., Turnbull, A. P., Turnbull, H. R., III, Wickham, D., Reuf, M., & Wilcox, B. (2000). Applying positive behavioral support and functional behavioral assessment in schools. *Journal of Positive Behavioral Interventions, 2*, 131–143.

Taylor-Greene, S., Brown, D., Nelson, L., Longton, J., Gassman, T., Cohen, J., Swartz, J., Horner, R. H., Sugai, G., & Hall, S. (1997). School-wide behavioral support: Starting the year off right. *Journal of Behavioral Education, 7*, 99–112.

Tobin, T., Sugai, G., & Colvin, G. (2000). Using discipline referrals to make decisions. *National Association of Secondary School Principals (NASSP), 84*(616) 106–117.

Tobin, T., Sugai, G., & Martin, E. (2000). *Final report for Project CREDENTIALS: Current research on educational endeavors to increase at-risk learners' success* (Report submitted to the Office of Professional Technical Education, Oregon Department of Education). Eugene, OR: University of Oregon, College of Education, Behavioral Research, and Teaching.

Todd, A. W., Horner, R. H., Sugai, G., & Sprague, J. R. (1999). Effective behavior support: Strengthening school-wide systems through a team-based approach. *Effective School Practices, 17*(4), 23–37.

U.S. Department of Health and Human Services (2001). *Youth violence: A report of the surgeon general—Executive summary.* Rockville, MD: U.S. Department of Health and Human Services, Centers for Disease Control and Prevention, National Center for Injury Prevention and Control; Substance Abuse and Mental Health Services Administration, Center for Mental Health Services; and National Institutes of Health.

U.S. Departments of Justice and Education. (1998). *First annual report on school safety.* Washington, D.C.: Author.

U.S. Departments of Justice and Education. (1999). *Annual report on school safety.* Washington, D.C.: Author.

U.S. Departments of Justice and Education. (2000). *Annual report on school safety.* Washington, D.C.: Author.

Vance, J., Fernandez, G., & Biber, M. (1998). Educational progress in a population of youth with aggression and emotional disturbance: The role of risk and protective factors. *Journal of Emotional and Behavioral Disorders, 6*(4), 214–221.

Walker, H. M. (1995). *The acting-out child: Coping with classroom disruption,* (2nd ed.) Longmont, CO: Sopris West Educational Services.

Walker, H. M. (1998). First steps to prevent antisocial behavior. *Teaching Exceptional Children, 30*(4), 16–19.

Walker, H. M., Colvin, G., & Ramsey, E. (1995). *Antisocial behavior in school: Strategies and best practices*. Pacific Grove, CA: Brooks/Cole.

Walker, H. M., Horner, R. H., Sugai, G., Bullis, M., Sprague, J. R., Bricker, D., & Kaufman, M. J. (1996). Integrated approaches to preventing antisocial behavior patterns among school-age children and youth. *Journal of Emotional and Behavioral Disorders, 4*(4), 194–209.

Walker, H. M., Stieber, S., Ramsey, E., & O'Neill, R. E. (1993). Fifth grade school adjustment and later arrest rate: A longitudinal study of middle school antisocial boys. *Journal of Child and Family Studies, 2*(4), 295–315.

Walker, H. M., & Walker, J. E. (1991). *Coping with noncompliance in the classroom: A positive approach for teachers*. Austin, TX: PRO-ED.

Webster-Stratton, C., & Herbert, M. (1994). *Troubled families: Problem children*. New York: John Wiley & Sons.

Wright, J. A., & Dusek, J. B. (1998). Research into practice: Compiling school base rates for disruptive behaviors from student disciplinary referral data. *School Psychology Review, 27*(1), 138–147.